AMERICAN
MUSIC LEGENDS

★★★

Includes personal stories shared by friends, family

and those who loved them

———— ★★★ ————

Photography   Les Leverett

Editor   Rob Simbeck

Creative Direction   McClearen Design Studios, Nashville, TN

Publisher   Cumberland Records

Cracker Barrel
Old Country Store®

Published by Cumberland Records
℗© 2005 CB Music, LLC. Produced and Manufactured for Cracker Barrel Old Country Store®
Printed in the United States of America

Les Leverett

photo by Dot Leverett

Les Leverett was the official photographer of the Grand Ole Opry from 1960 until his retirement in 1992. His photographs have appeared on numerous album and CD covers, in books, magazines and TV documentaries. His awards include a Grammy for the cover of Porter Wagoner's 1966 album, "Confessions of a Broken Man," a 1972 Billboard magazine award for Best Country Music Album Cover for Dolly Parton's "Bubbling Over," a "Walkway of Stars" in 1994, a Distinguished Achievement Award from the International Bluegrass Music Association in 2001 and the Reunion of Professional Entertainers Media Person Award in 2004.

Born in Montgomery, Alabama, in 1927, and raised in southern Alabama, Les served in the U.S. Army during and after World War II. He became interested in photography at an early age and studied under the G.I. Bill in San Antonio, Texas, where he met his wife of 56 years, Nashville native, Dorothy Vandiver, who was working for The National Life & Accident Insurance Company, owners and operatiors of WSM radio and the Grand Ole Opry. They moved to Nashville in 1950 and Les went to work for National Life, WSM, WSM-TV, and the Opry in 1960.

Les has two sons (one deceased) and a daughter who is a photographer and author. He and Dorothy live happily in Goodlettsville, Tennessee.

Contributors

Bill Anderson is a member of the the Grand Ole Opry and of the Country Music Hall of Fame.

Keith Bilbrey is an air personality on WSM-AM in Nashville and a staff announcer and lifelong fan of the Grand Ole Opry.

Jonathan Burchfield is an accomplished classical guitarist and tours with his brother, Benji Burchfield, who plays mallet kat. They are known as The Burchfield Brothers. www.burchfieldbrothers.com

Craig Campbell is vice-president of press and publicity for Sony Music Nashville.

Carlene Carter is a singer and actor who is a third-generation member of the legendary Carter Family. She is the daughter of June Carter Cash and Carl Smith.

John Carter Cash is a record producer and the son of Johnny Cash and June Carter Cash.

Charlie Chase has hosted or co-hosted "This Week In Country Music," "The Crook and Chase Show," and many other television and radio programs.

Cowboy Jack Clement worked as a producer and engineer at Sun Records, produced Charley Pride, owned one of Nashville's premiere studios and has written a number of hit songs.

Libby Leverett-Crew, the daughter of Les Leverett, is an artist, photographer, writer, and the author of *Saturday Nights with Daddy* at the Opry (Rutledge Hill Press). She lives in Nashville with her husband and daughter.

Bill Cody has been the morning host at WSM-AM in Nashville for 11 years. He hosts "GAC Classic" and the United Airlines "Authentic Sounds" channel, and has done a great deal of other TV and radio hosting and voiceover work.

Charlie Dick was a record promoter and video producer. He was the husband of the late Patsy Cline.

Bob DiPiero is a songwriter whose hits include "If You Ever Stop Loving Me," "American Made," "Daddy's Money" and "Blue Clear Sky."

Jessy Dixon is one of the world's most renowned gospel singers. He has worked with Mahalia Jackson and Paul Simon, and he is currently part of the Gaither Homecoming Tour.

Ranger Douglas B. Green is a music historian, an award-winning Western music songwriter, and lead and baritone singer of Riders in the Sky.

Schatzi Hageman is a celebrity press agent.

Claude Hall was radio-TV editor of *Billboard* for 14 years. He is a college professor, a writer, and an enduring fan.

Stan Hitchcock is CEO of BlueHighways TV. He was the host of the long-running, nationally syndicated "Stan Hitchcock Show."

David Holt is a musician, storyteller, four-time Grammy Award winner, and host of the PBS *Folkways* series and National Public Radio's *Riverwalk*.

Kathy Hughes is the daughter of Cowboy Copas.

Ramona Jones "As a longtime performer on the Grand Ole Opry I met many great entertainers and feel that they became 'my people.'"

Larry Jordan is the author of "Jim Reeves: His Untold Story"

Buddy Killen is CEO of the Killen Music Group. He is past owner of the legendary Tree International music publishing company.

Bob Kingsley is host and producer of *American Country Countdown with Bob Kingsley*

Bill Littleton is a life-long resident of the American South. He helped invent freelance entertainment journalism in Nashville, having had a thousand bylines in *Performance* magazine alone and an estimated that many more collectively in other publications.

Loretta Lynn is a member of the Country Music Hall of Fame.

Kathy Mattea was twice the CMA Female Vocalist of the Year.

William R. "Billy" Maxwell is golf professional at Fall Creek Falls State Park in Pikeville, TN. On the road with Riders in the Sky, he is "merchandise salesman and Woody Paul's handler."

Dean Miller is a singer and songwriter. He is the son of Roger Miller.

Michael Montana is the grandson of Patsy Montana.

Susan Nadler is executive vice-president of Bandit Records.

John Riggs is a songwriter/entertainer who came to Nashville back when country music.........was. His biggest thrill has been meeting all those recording artists whom he admired growing up and having many of them record his songs.

Dave Salyer was the lead guitarist with Barbara Mandrell's band the Do-Rites.

Rob Simbeck's work has appeared in *The Washington Post, Rolling Stone, Country Weekly, Guideposts,* and many other publications. Rob is Nashville Bureau Chief of the syndicated radio show *American Country Countdown with Bob Kingsley.*

Ricky Skaggs has won eight CMA awards, including "Entertainer of the Year," ten Grammys, and many other awards. He is one of bluegrass music's most formidable artists.

The Southern Gentlemen—Gary Robble, Lin Bown, and Glenn Huggins—toured and recorded with Sonny James from 1964-1971.

Gordon Stoker is first tenor and manager of the Jordanaires.

Marty Stuart toured as a member of the bands of both Lester Flatt and Johnny Cash. He has released half a dozen successful albums of his own.

Eddie Stubbs is a disc jockey at WSM-AM and a staff announcer at the Grand Ole Opry.

Sonny Throckmorton is a songwriter whose many hits include "Why Not Me," "The Way I Am," and "Middle Age Crazy."

Anastasia ("Anna") Morgan Trainor is the widow of George Morgan.

Frederick "B" Townes is Dean of Development, Wilkes Community College, and MerleFest founder.

Bob Tubert has been a songwriter, artist manager, producer, and Music Row catalyst.

Porter Wagoner is a member of the Grand Ole Opry and of the Country Music Hall of Fame.

Alisa Jones Wall is a legendary hammered dulcimer player and the daughter of Grandpa Jones.

Cindy Wills is the youngest daughter of Bob Wills.

Chely Wright's hits include "Single White Female," "Shut Up and Drive" and "The Bumper of My S.U.V." Her "Reading, Writing and Rhythm" charitable foundation has raised more than a million dollars to provide musical instruments for underfunded public school music programs.

Billy Yates is a singer and songwriter whose credits include "I Don't Need Your Rocking Chair" and "Choices."

Bill Anderson, page 12 and 30, reprinted with permission from *I Hope You're Living As High On The Hog As The Pig You Turned Out To Be* by Bill Anderson. © 1994, TWI, Inc.
Loretta Lynn, page 36, reprinted with permission from *You're Cookin' It Country* by Loretta Lynn. © 2004, Rutledge Hill Press.
Marty Stuart, page 124, reprinted with permission from *Pilgrims—Sinners, Saints and Prophets* by Marty Stuart.
© 1999 Rutledge Hill Press.

Roy Acuff
★ ★ ★

After 20 years in Illinois, Mark, Benji and I (The Burchfield Brothers) decided to return to our home state of Tennessee. With our bags packed and instruments loaded, we set our sights on becoming part of the music community in Nashville. Somewhere along the way, the car began filling with smoke. I looked at Mark, sleeping in the back, and saw smoke rising from Mark's Levi's. I said, "Mark! Wake up! I think you're on fire!" We stopped and put him out, then discovered the seat was burning beneath him due to a ruptured exhaust pipe. We put it out and all got in the front seat, since there was nothing left in the back but ashes. Weary from the trip, we entered Nashville and pulled to the side of the road in our half-burned car. We were looking at a map when a beautiful Cadillac pulled in front of us, and out stepped this old gentleman with wavy silver hair. He wiped the sweat from his forehead as he slowly walked up to our car. When he said, "Can I help you boys?" we realized we were talking to Roy Acuff, the King of Country Music. We said we'd just moved to town, and he encouraged us to be faithful to Christ and find a good church. I then told him we were musicians.

"I know," he replied. "I can tell by your car."

—Jonathan Burchfield

In 1981, friends and admirers from all over the country gathered at Nashville's Hyatt Regency Hotel to honor Roy for his life and his accomplishments as a singer, musician, music publisher, and actor. They included Johnny Cash, June Carter, Minnie Pearl and, at the head table, vice-president and Mrs. George Bush and Mr. and Mrs. Gene Autry. Roy was roasted royally, something that he really enjoyed. The festivities included a reception at the governor's mansion and a private party at the Hyatt following the roast. As I was leaving the last party, I spotted Roy and I went over to congratulate him. He asked where I had been, saying he hadn't seen me at the Opry in a while. I told him that, sadly, my mother had passed away and that we had been in Alabama for a week. We had come home for a day, then driven to Colorado for a week's vacation and to pick up our daughter Libby, who was finishing a summer of work there. I mentioned that it had been a tough couple of weeks.

Roy looked me right in the eye and asked, "Do you need any money?" "No," I replied, "but God bless you, Roy. I'll never forget you for asking me." I was astounded. Here was a man who had spent the day being honored by a crowd of people including the governor and vice-president, and he was humble enough to think of someone else and see if he couldn't help with their journey.

—Les Leverett, told to Libby Leverett-Crew

ROY ACUFF

★ ★ ★ ★ ★

1907—1995

photo taken October 1980

Bill Anderson

★ ★ ★

I met Bill Anderson the night President Richard Nixon appeared at the grand opening of the new Grand Ole Opry House in 1974. Later, as I went to work for WSM-AM and eventually became an Opry announcer, Bill was a colleague and treasured friend, one for whom my respect and admiration have grown greatly through the years. He is someone who's quick with a joke, someone I can sit with just to talk about our kids or a bachelor's secret to making corn bread. He has also been there for me through my divorce, a car accident, and the deaths of mutual friends. Perhaps he never meant more to me than the night my dear friend and mentor, Opry announcer Grant Turner, died. I idolized Grant. His death was sudden and unexpected, and I heard about it as I pulled onto the exit ramp to the Opry House for a show. I was still in a state of shock as we went on the air with *Grand Ole Opry Live on TNN.* I knew I was going to have to say something on the air that night, and I knew it was going to be difficult. The time came, and as I faced that television audience I began stumbling my way through an emotional speech about Grant and his death. It was all I could do to get it out. As I did, I noticed someone standing beside the camera I was addressing. It was Bill Anderson, but in that white suit, with a look of compassion on his face, I swear for a second he looked like an angel. He knew I was having a hard time and he was there, gently supporting me. When I was finished, I walked to him and buried my head in his chest. That moment meant more to me than I could ever say.

—Keith Bilbrey

When I was in grade school, I discovered that I liked to sing, and the older I got, the more I did it. I liked some rock, pop, and country, but then the people in rock and pop started looking like throwbacks to the Neanderthal man and the lyrics became an insult to my ears. So I decided to buy some country albums and tune everyone else out. Shortly after that decision, I told myself I was going to be a country singer. My problem was that I didn't know how to get started.

At this point I was in the military, and I had the great idea of writing to four or five country singers in care of the Grand Ole Opry to ask for some advice. I don't remember the names of all those I wrote to, but I do remember that only one of them took the time to answer with a typewritten letter, giving me his personal tips on how I might get started. I was thrilled to get that letter and it made me feel like I was practically an Opry member, and that I had a friend in Nashville, even though I wouldn't get to meet him until several years after I arrived here.

This encouraging letter is one of the reasons I had the nerve to come to Nashville with less than thirty dollars and no job in sight. I didn't worry too much because I knew Bill Anderson. And, Bill, if by chance you're reading this story, I still have among my most prized possessions your letter...... dated 1-15-64.

—John Riggs

BILL ANDERSON

1937—

photo taken 1961

Louis Armstrong

★ ★ ★

He was a founding father of jazz, casting a shadow over all that would follow, and he made millions of dollars, but Louis Armstrong and his wife Lucille would live from the early '40s in a modest house in a racially mixed working-class neighborhood in Queens. In fact, Louis, who for decades played an average of 300 nights a year on the road, was traveling when Lucille bought the house, and he returned to it sight unseen. She had known the neighborhood since she was a child and liked its feel—neighborhood kids would watch TV and eat ice cream with Louis; Lucille would take food to neighbors when their family members died; Louis would play his trumpet from a tiny balcony off his den. He could have afforded to live anywhere, but he said, "We don't think we could be more relaxed and have better neighbors anyplace else," and he lived there until his death in 1971.

—Rob Simbeck

I was eating lunch in a little restaurant with a friend of mine in 1970 when Louis Armstrong came on the TV. My friend had known Louis since he was a kid, and he said, "Why don't we get him into the studio to cut a country record?" I thought it was a great idea, and Louis did too, so we got together in a studio in New York with a band I put together. I had sent him 26 songs to pick 12 from—covers like "Running Bear" and "Almost Persuaded," and a song I wrote called "Why Did Mrs. Murphy Leave Town?" —and I asked if he liked any of them. "I love them all," he said, so I'd just pick one and we'd start cutting. I had Larry Butler playing piano, and Louis sat on the bench with Larry and they ran down the first song and then Louis walked over to the microphone. Well, the first time he sang it, it sounded just awful, and I thought, "What have I gotten myself into here?" But then the second time he sang it, he nailed it. He did it that way every time. That's when I understood him, because he was doing something I used to do. He was just messing with the song the first time through, feeling it out, getting all the mistakes out of the way up front. Then, when you're warmed up, you take it seriously. He was somebody I really enjoyed. He was a dream to work with, just like you'd expect him to be, the way he was on TV or in the movies. He didn't have to think about playing a role. He *was* a role. He was Louis. People loved him because he was set free in himself.

—Cowboy Jack Clement, told to Rob Simbeck

LOUIS ARMSTRONG

★ ★ ★ ★ ★

1900—1971

photo taken 1970

Eddy Arnold

★ ★ ★

I was sitting in Eddy Arnold's office in Franklin, TN, finishing up an interview for *American Country Countdown with Bob Kingsley.* After I had turned off the tape, we kept shooting the breeze about music. He was telling stories about events that had happened as long as 60 years ago, stories he had surely told many times before. Still, his energy and fervor made them seem like it was the first time. He was, after all, talking about songs—writing them, singing them, recording them. I told him about my mother, who had been through serious surgery and who had asked me to send good wishes and tell him how much she loved his version of the song "Have I Told You Lately That I Love You?"

"I just re-recorded that with a wonderful duet partner," he said, brightening even more. "Let me make your mother a copy." And at that, he began looking through tapes and firing up tape decks. I watched as one of the biggest stars of the 20th century made my mother a copy of the thing with his own hands, talking about the duet partner and his new recordings all the while.

Eddy Arnold invested his money wisely and he is a millionaire many times over. He is *Billboard* magazine's #1 country artist *of all time* based on airplay, with chart hits spread over five decades. He has nothing to prove to anyone. And yet in his '80s, it remained all about the music and its effect on people, one person at a time. The personal touch he showed with me and with my mother is one you could always hear in his voice, and it was that quality, as much as any, that resonated with people and made him the legend he remains.

—Rob Simbeck

Eddy Arnold has long been recognized as one of country music's most astute businessmen. In the late '50s, he went into the real estate business in the then rural community of Brentwood, south of Nashville. Not only did Eddy buy up much of the lush, rolling farmland that would later be sold to housing developers, but he also was the guiding force behind the formation of the Brentwood Water Company.

In later years, many country music stars would move to Brentwood and receive their water from Eddy's company. One of these was Tom T. Hall, who moved into the palatial Fox Hollow estate.

"It really makes me mad," Tom T. said one day, grinning as he spoke. "Every time I flush my toilet, Eddy Arnold makes a nickel!"

—Bill Anderson

EDDY ARNOLD

★★★★★

1918—

photo taken 1960

Chet Atkins
★ ★ ★

Chet could never figure out why some people felt intimidated by him. He was one of the mildest, meekest souls anywhere, but he was such a formidable figure, such a legend, that people would be afraid of him. He and Connie Smith were on my show once, and she said how intimidated she had been when she first got to town, and he just couldn't understand it. As an interview, Chet was a really understated guy. He had a dry, self-deprecating delivery that made his story-telling that much better. I always just wanted to hang on every word when he'd talk. He was on the television show *Prime Time Country* one night and he started talking about his early life, and I didn't realize just how tragic it had been. His father came in one day and just kind of announced, "Kiddies, I'm gone. I'm leaving." And he just left them. Chet told it so well, so beautifully and so tragically, that I guess I must have looked like I was going to cry. He said, "It's OK, Bill. No need to be so upset. It all worked out like it was supposed to." Obviously, at that point it affected me a lot more than it did him.

—Bill Cody, told to Rob Simbeck

There's an old tale about people asking Chet, "Just what is the Nashville Sound?" Well, he had helped create it, and when they'd ask he just reached in his pocket and jingled his change.

—Eddie Stubbs

Chet last recorded for Columbia Records, and about the time "The Day The Fingerpickers Took Over The World" or "Almost Alone" came out, he came to speak to the employees at a company retreat. It was an incredible thrill for all of us to be sitting with a man we basically knew as a master guitar player. He gave us an autobiographical snapshot of his life, particularly his early years and his start in music, and what we saw was an incredibly humble man with a hilarious, dry sense of humor. He'd talk about getting a radio job somewhere, give us a description of it, and say, "I got fired from that one." Then he'd talk about his next job, and say, "I got fired from that one too." He did that several times and his whole demeanor was that he himself was surprised that he ever amounted to anything because he just kept getting fired from jobs. He hung out with us for quite a while that afternoon, and he really treated us all like family. By the end of the session the feeling for me was that I was just sitting there talking with a friend. It wasn't until he left that I thought, "That was Chet Atkins!", somebody who had worked with everybody as a label head, who helped create the Nashville Sound, who discovered so many superstars, and who influenced everybody who ever picked up a guitar afterwards. It was really magical.

—Craig Campbell, told to Rob Simbeck

CHET ATKINS

★ ★ ★ ★ ★

1924 — 2001

photo taken 1977

Gene Autry
★ ★ ★

There is only one entertainer with five stars on Hollywood's Walk of Fame, and Gene Autry is the one. Those stars honor his accomplishments in radio, records, film, television, and live theatrical and rodeo performances. In an era of major cowboy stars, he was the biggest, making 90+ movies and singing classics like "Back In The Saddle Again," "Here Comes Santa Claus," and "Rudolph, The Red-Nosed Reindeer." He went on to become a highly successful businessman and an important figure in Hollywood. More than a decade after his death, the accolades continue: in 2005, the intersection of Hollywood & Highland was dedicated as Gene Autry Square.

—Rob Simbeck

Gene Autry and his wife Jackie paid a visit to the Grand Ole Opry in February 1983. We all gathered in Roy Acuff's dressing room to make photographs with various Opry members and friends. Mrs. Autry kept looking at me and then finally told me that I looked familiar to her. I reminded her that we had met a couple of years earlier when they were in town for the roasting of Roy Acuff. She had not seen the photos that were taken that evening and wanted me to send her copies. She gave me an address in Palm Springs, California. Gene owned a hotel there, although they lived in Los Angeles. I told her that my wife Dot and I were going to be in Palm Springs the following spring and how much we were looking forward to visiting the area again. Later, I sent the Autrys photographs from the Acuff roast and from that February night at the Opry. Spring came, and we went on our trip to Palm Springs, and when we returned to Nashville, we found in our mail a thank-you note from Gene. He had added a note that said, "Call me when you are in Palm Springs." That was a high honor to me, although it had arrived after our trip. I received another letter from Gene not long after the first. It was typed and signed in brown ink. He said he was very grateful for the photographs I had made and sent, and I really did feel like we could indeed just call him up when we were in Palm Springs. I consider those notes from Gene Autry some of my most prized possessions.

—Les Leverett, told to Libby Leverett-Crew

GENE AUTRY

★★★★★

1907—1998

photo taken 1983

Count Basie

★ ★ ★

In February of 1961, Count Basie was in town to appear on *The Noon Show*, which aired on WSM's sister television station, WSMV. Count was a good friend of WSMV promotion man Charlie Cash, who wasn't able to get away to transport Count from his motel to the station. Instead, Charlie sent a young man in his place, and asked if I would go with him and cover the story. It is sad to think that less than 50 years ago, Count Basie was not allowed to stay in a motel close to the TV station simply because of the color of his skin. Well, the young man and I drove over to his motel off of Clarksville Highway, north of Nashville. Count was a very likeable man, and the three of us carried on a lively, fun conversation on the way back into town.

I made my photographs during the show, trying to cover it from every angle. At one point, I went into the control room and photographed out over the engineer's shoulders so as to capture the controls in the foreground and Judd Collins talking with Count Basie in the studio beyond. It was then that I overheard one of the engineers remark, "I wish you would listen to the voice on that guy. He makes us sound like Mickey Mouse." Well, that wasn't true, of course, but Count did have one of the most beautiful, resonant voices I've ever heard. I've always admired Count Basie, and was very proud to be in his presence that day.

—Les Leverett, told to Libby Leverett-Crew

When he was a boy, William Basie helped out at the Palace Theater in Red Bank, New Jersey, in order to get in for free. He worked a spotlight during Vaudeville shows and learned to run the movie projectors. He had been taking piano lessons—at 25 cents a piece—and one day when the theater's piano player, who accompanied the otherwise silent films, couldn't make it in, Basie asked the manager if he could fill in. The manager said no, but Basie eased over to the piano and began playing anyway. He did well enough that he earned an invitation to come back and do it again that evening. It was the beginning of a lifetime of music-making. Basie would be established on the Vaudeville circuit himself while still a teenager, and by his early '30s, his Count Basie Orchestra was one of the nation's finest and best-known big bands. His orchestra included a Who's Who of jazz musicians and vocalists, and Basie was widely regarded as a man always willing to share the spotlight and credit when it came to music. His 60-year career was one of the century's most important.

—Rob Simbeck

Count Basie

★ ★ ★ ★ ★

1904—1984

photo taken 1961

Tony Bennett
★ ★ ★

Song stylist, humanitarian, supporter of environmental concerns and artist, Tony Bennett is not only an amazing entertainer; he is an amazing human being. Born Anthony Dominick Benedetto in Queens, New York, he changed his name at the suggestion of Bob Hope, who discovered Tony and his singing talents while listening to him perform with Pearl Bailey in Greenwich Village in the late '40s.

In 1990, while photographing a convention at the Opryland Hotel in Nashville, I was delighted to find that the organization that had hired my services had also hired Tony Bennett as their special entertainment for the evening. I was asked to get a few photos of Mr. Bennett with the organization's executives. I suggested to his representative that we hold this photo session before the show, before Mr. Bennett became exhausted. The young lady informed me that "Mr. Bennett does not become exhausted." She was not kidding. He put on a grand show that evening, which included projections of his paintings. As soon as he began "I Left My Heart In San Francisco," I knew that he was wrapping up his act, so I got a head start to the room where the photo session was to take place. I was quite surprised to find him waiting when I arrived. He knew about the freight elevator. I did not. There was no one else in the room except his assistant, who was sitting in the corner on the phone, so I introduced myself to Mr. Bennett and took a seat close by.

Indeed, he was not exhausted. He began talking, and somehow he ended up telling me about how he had just left Las Vegas, where he had done a benefit with what was left of the Rat Pack for the retired musicians' fund. He was very interested when I told him that we had a similar benefit in Nashville. Our visit was relaxed and enjoyable, as was the photo session.

A couple of weeks later, we were watching *The Tonight Show* and Tony Bennett was a guest. During his interview he told the same story about singing for the musician's benefit in Las Vegas, then went on to tell Jay Leno about how there was a similar organization in Nashville. It's the closest I've come to being on *The Tonight Show*.

—Les Leverett, told to Libby Leverett-Crew

TONY BENNETT

★★★★★

1926—

photo taken 1990

George Burns

★ ★ ★

George was just a wonderful man. I met him at Gene Autry's 82nd birthday party in L.A., and one other time, and when he came to the Opry for an appearance later I didn't know if he would remember me. He came back to my dressing room and someone said, "Do you know Porter Wagoner?" and he said, "I've known him all my life." Of course, it was me that had known about him all my life because I'd seen him going back to the days of his TV show. He was really friendly and of course everybody who saw him knew who he was. He was a brilliant man and I had a great visit with him. He was a great guy to talk to because he knew about everything that went on in the music business back to the beginning. Of course, he was close to 100 years old at the time, but he went out and told three or four jokes on stage that night for the Opry audience. He was a magical man.

—Porter Wagoner, told to Rob Simbeck

I published "I Wish I Was 18 Again," which Sonny Throckmorton had written and Jerry Lee Lewis had a hit on. George Burns decided to cut the song again, and they put a band together for him and did everything live, with no overdubs. I went over for the session and he was just one of the sweetest guys. I was standing there and he said, "Come on over and sit down," and all of us felt really comfortable with him. He had absolutely no attitude, but then, you know, most of the mature ones don't. I had been around a couple of those Hollywood folks who didn't know what humility was, but he was a very humble guy, It was nice to see in someone who had been around as long as he had.

—Buddy Killen, told to Rob Simbeck

Being around George was always thoroughly enjoyable. He was one of the guys, and someone who was on all the time. He was also from the old school, and really respectful of creative people. He had been a great writer all his life, and so he knew what was involved.

I went out to California once to pitch George a song to follow up, "I Wish I Was 18 Again." When I got there, I called his house and got word he was at a TV studio taping either the Merv Griffin or Mike Douglas show. He invited me to come to the studio, so I did, and as we were sitting in the dressing room he asked if I'd go on with him and pitch the song on the air. It was a pretty unusual request, but I borrowed Hoyt Axton's guitar—Hoyt was on before George—and got ready to go out. As we were waiting, George looked and me and deadpanned, "If you'll excuse me, I've got to go to the bathroom, and I'd rather do it in here than on the stage." A few minutes later, I pitched him the song live on the air and he wound up recording it.

—Sonny Throckmorton

GEORGE BURNS

★★★★★

1896—1996

photo taken 1980

Glen Campbell
★ ★ ★

Glen Campbell was the quintessential small-town-boy-makes-good story, a Delight, Arkansas, kid who rode talent and drive to the biggest recording studios in Los Angeles. He played for Sinatra, Dean Martin, Merle Haggard, the Beach Boys, and countless others before climbing his own way to the top. And then, after years of fast lanes, he still had a touch of Delight in him. He was doing a session with Jan and Dean when he first heard Jimmy Webb's "By The Time I Get To Phoenix." "I don't know if it was the bird flying out of the ashes or what," he told me, "but when I heard the song I cried, because I was homesick. I was in L.A. and I had driven that route before." He selected songs with his gut and when they had an emotional effect on him, they would invariably have it on the public. His stardom had no less an effect on him, and it was instantaneous. He did two episodes of *The Summer Brothers Smothers Show*, went to England for a quick promotional tour, and came back to find that everyone in the airport—and in the country—seemed to know who he was all at once. There are pitfalls to such stardom, as episodes in his life have proven, but there would be no disputing the talent inside the so-recently homesick smalltown boy, the level of stardom he would sustain, or the contributions he has made to popular music.

—Rob Simbeck

Not all entertainers are willing to take the time and energy to help newer acts, but Glen is one of those that is. When I worked shows with him, he was always very gracious, and he would always check out the opening acts. It's almost like he remained a sideman at heart, someone who wanted to study the musicians, to see how good they were. He would be that way on flights to shows, too, pulling out a guitar to play with everybody on the way.

There are famous examples of the way his help made a difference. One goes back to *The Glen Campbell Goodtime Hour*, when he brought John Hartford out of obscurity and made him a regular on the show. Then there was the time Alan Jackson's wife approached him in an airport to tell him about her struggling songwriting husband and Glen directed her to his Nashville publisher, giving Alan a start on his rise to stardom. It's a quality that has meant a lot to quite a few people over the years.

—Bob Tubert, told to Rob Simbeck

GLEN CAMPBELL

★★★★★

1932—

photo taken 1983

The Carter Family
★ ★ ★

As the Opry's photographer, I worked with Maybelle, Helen, June and Anita all the time, and all of them lived not far from us in Madison, Tennessee. In fact, we bought a house back in the 1950s and when we got a copy of the deed, we found that Maybelle Carter had owned and lived in the house at one time. Our children were friends and we had mutual friends in the neighborhood. My wife Dot, my daughter Libby and I went by the home of our friends Cecil and Annette Null one night to pay a call and found them and Maybelle sitting in the kitchen playing a card game called PoKeNo. They asked us to join them, and since this was a penny-ante game, Dot dug around in her purse and found a few pennies so we could play with them. Maybelle had a pretty good stash of pennies, maybe a good handful, sitting in front of her, and Dot commenced to win every one of them. All these years later, Dot still has that little jar of pennies she won off Maybelle.

We loved that blue-eyed Maybelle and all of those girls. It's sad to think they are all gone now, but they certainly left a lot of happiness in their wake.

—Les Leverett, told to Libby Leverett-Crew

Mother Maybelle was a guest on my television show, *The Porter Wagoner Show,* quite a few times, and people just loved her. I also had her and the girls on–June and Anita and Helen. You could feel the spirit of those early days of the Carter Family, of their place in the legacy of country music, whenever they were on. Maybelle could be quiet but we had some good conversations on camera. I remember once telling her how my dad, when he was singing a song, would sing lead one line, then tenor one line, and bass another line, and she said that A.P. would do that too. I also asked her about the recordings where he wouldn't sing all the time, where he'd come in and out vocally, and she said a lot of times he would just walk through the room as they were recording, sing a little bit and walk on by. I got to know quite a bit about him and about the family during those shows.

—Porter Wagoner, told to Rob Simbeck

THE CARTER FAMILY

★★★★★

Valerie June Carter Cash 1929—2003, Anita Carter 1933—1999,
Helen Myrl Carter Jones 1927—1998, Maybelle Addington Carter 1909—1978

photo taken 1965

June Carter

★ ★ ★

My father had a brain aneurism and he had to have surgery, so he was in intensive care at Baptist Hospital. Johnny Cash had just had heart surgery, and I was in the hall one day as June came by. "Who have you got in there?" she asked me and I told her it was my daddy. She asked if he was doing OK and I said, "Yeah, but he's pretty banged up." Well, she went in to see him and out of all the people who came and went, he knew June Carter. From then on, every morning when she came to see Johnny she stopped by and had prayer with my father. And every time I saw her after that she asked, "How's your daddy doing?" and she kept up with that until her dying day.

—**Keith Bilbrey**

I came to Nashville in 1951 and worked with the Carters a lot. They were a sweet and wonderful group of people. June was a really funny, funny character, and that's what most people saw when they looked at her. I was lucky enough to see her from another vantage point, getting into a lot of serious conversations with her over the years. She was very philosophical in her own country way, and the things she said even when she was trying to be funny had real substance to them. I've always thought that every comedian wants to do something serious, and she sure had the thoughtful, intellectual side to prove that. She was a very smart woman, and she was one of a kind.

—**Buddy Killen, told to Rob Simbeck**

When I was living in England many years ago, Mama got sick one time. I kept calling her and she'd sound so awful on the phone. "I've got pneumonia," she told me. I called every day for a week and she sounded worse every day. Finally I started thinking about going home to be with her.

Then one day at the end of the week I got John on the phone and I asked how Mama was doing.

"She's made a miraculous recovery," he said.

"What happened?" I asked him.

"She's down on a movie set with Robert Duvall." She had gone down to hang out with the man she called "Bobbie." The next day I called again and she was back to being her sick self on the phone and I said, "Mama, I've been worried to death and you were out running around a movie set."

"Well, Bobbie came into town and he needed me," she said.

"But you had pneumonia!"

"Well," she said sheepishly, "I guess it was walking pneumonia."

Mama was addicted to cheesecake—ordered it in bulk from the Cheesecake Factory—but it wasn't until just a year or two before she died that she realized there were places that would bring pizzas to your house. I was living in Mama and John's house at the time, and John was in the hospital off and on that year. She and I would get in her bed and watch old movies, and she would say, "I know what we need! We need pizza!" And if I was depressed, she'd say, "I need a piece of cheesecake and you could use a pizza." So lots of times the delivery guy would have to come in through the gate and past the guard and come into the house with pizza because Mama had learned about home delivery.

—**Carlene Carter, told to Rob Simbeck**

JUNE CARTER

★★★★★

1929—2003

photo taken 1970

Johnny Cash

My dad grew up listening to the radio. He never thought about going on the road necessarily or even putting out a record. What he wanted to do was be on the radio. He got that inspiration from artists like Eddy Arnold, Jimmie Rodgers and the Carter Family.

His great love early on was gospel music, and it was that way throughout his life, actually. He wanted to be a gospel singer, but he had this strong, dark character to his voice, and when Sam Phillips heard him audition with a song like "I Was There When It Happened" or "Belshazzar," he said, "I don't want a gospel act. Go back and write an up-tempo love song and come back," and dad came back with "Cry, Cry Cry," and "Hey Porter."

Sam signed him and he earned an important place in the history of music. He was part of rock 'n roll from the beginning. My dad became a voice for the common man—a strong, dark but spiritual voice, honest and direct. His backing music was simple, almost archaic, but perfect in its own way. It was a sound that had never been heard before. No one has been able to successfully copy it since.

—John Carter Cash, told to Rob Simbeck

Johnny and I were staying at the same hotel the night a dirty, stray dog followed him off the street and into the lobby through a revolving door. "Get that awful dog out of here!" the bellman roared. "Don't you touch my dog," Johnny bellowed right back. "Oh, Mr. Cash, I'm so sorry. I didn't realize this was your dog. Please accept my apologies." John, of course, had never seen the dog before in his life, but he and his band members played the scene to the hilt. They took the dog upstairs, gave it a bath and tucked it into bed. Next morning, I heard they had ordered two dozen hamburgers at midnight.

—Bill Anderson

The last time I saw Johnny was at Sam's, where he frequently shopped. Not wanting to draw attention to him and his daughter, Rosanne, I held the palm of my right hand up from my waist and just wiggled my fingers at him. He nodded, acknowledging that he had seen me. He was wearing light-colored pants and a white shirt, and he looked less like the Man in Black that day than I had ever seen him. It was almost like he had dressed to go home.

—Les Leverett, told to Libby Leverett-Crew

JOHNNY CASH

★ ★ ★ ★ ★

1932—2003

photo taken 1970

Ray Charles

★★★

The first time I ever had co-billing with a blues artist was at a blues fest with Bobby "Blue" Bland in Milwaukee. A secular agency had booked me to a series of shows, and at the next one, in Mobile, there was Ray Charles. I'll never forget, first of all because they all came out on stage in pink tuxedos. I remember him talking to his musicians in between singing lines of songs. He really knew his craft, and his ears were like radar, and anytime somebody was flat or had missed a note he would pull back from the microphone and let them know it. The audience never knew it–all they heard was that wonderful singing of his. My mouth was open the whole time. I was just amazed at how he wanted everything so perfect.

He really liked the way my three female backup singers, the Jessy Dixon Singers, sounded. I thought, "Man, I hope he doesn't steal my group." He also spent a lot of time over in the corner talking to my piano player at the time, Elsa Harris, and I'm thinking, "There go my musicians too." I thought maybe someone had described her to him because she looked good too. But he was very nice to us and we had the greatest time together. He was like a teacher and he liked all forms of music. He loved country, and he had started out singing gospel quartet music, like the Swan Silvertones, the Dixie Hummingbirds and the Pilgrim Travelers, and his knowledge of gospel spilled over to what he was doing as a secular artist. He asked me how I could ever make it as a secular artist not crossing over like he had to do, but it wasn't a temptation for me. It wasn't like I was missing out on singing before big crowds–there I was with him!

—Jessy Dixon, told to Rob Simbeck

The guest list at Ray Charles' funeral was itself an indication of the breadth and depth of the influence he had on the world. B. B. King, Glen Campbell, Wynton Marsalis, Clint Eastwood and Willie Nelson all took part in memorializing him. The occasion inspired heights of music and oratory, with the emotional speech of Stevie Wonder one of the most moving. "Long before I knew we had so much in common," he said, "I knew him as a man and a voice that touched my heart. His voice made me feel like I wanted to love deeper, to care more and reach out and touch the world."

—Rob Simbeck

RAY CHARLES

★ ★ ★ ★ ★

1930—2004

photo taken 1970

Roy Clark
★ ★ ★

Roy Clark had cut my song, "The Tips Of My Fingers," in 1963 and had his first hit with it. I had cut it back in 1960. Then Steve Wariner cut it and had a Top 5 hit with it in 1992. Well, right after that, Steve and I were standing in the hallway backstage at the Opry, and here comes Roy Clark walking down the hall toward us. He doesn't look up, he doesn't say hello to either one of us. Now, you're thinking at a moment like that, that he might say, "Congratulations on your new success with the song," or at least, "Hello," or something, but no, Roy just keeps on walking by. But as he gets along side of us he says, with a perfect sense of timing, "I put it back in my act" and just kept on walking. Broke us both up.

—Bill Anderson, told to Rob Simbeck

Armed with jokes about how his hometown of Meherrin, Virginia, got its name, Roy Clark tackled the music business from so many fronts it took a while for some to catch on to just what he did. He's obviously a brilliant multi-instrumentalist whose vocal interpretations led to serious hit records, and a man whose comedic skills provided an anchor for all those years of *Hee Haw*, but the thing that made him a star is the natural down-home warmth that makes people want him to be successful. Of all the characters he's done on television, he does Roy Clark magnificently.

I had the opportunity to cover the early 1970s recording sessions Roy did with his father and the family band that had given birth to his amazing career. Nothing was updated, nothing altered for young audiences, nothing slicked up for Nashville Sound compatibility. They simply played the country music they had played when Roy was a youngster. From the days when they were invited to play for President Roosevelt on the lawn of the White House to the days when he became a highly commercial country star, selling lots of records, that authenticity remained the foundation of his career. In a much later interview, I asked him what country music meant to him. "In the first place," he replied with almost no pause, "it has to come from something. You can't just make it up. It has to have roots." And Roy Clark knows the roots of his music well.

—Bill Littleton

Grandpa and I were working for Connie B. Gay on WARL in Arlington, Virginia, when we first met Roy, probably in 1948 or 49. Grandpa had hired him for a date in Maryland, and that night the three of us were driving home. I said to Grandpa, "Didn't Roy do a great job tonight?" He said, "He sure did," and he turned around and said, "Roy, you've got a job with us if you want it. Can you start working with us in the morning?" and he did. A few years later he got married and I remember him laughingly asking us if we'd come to the wedding. He said, "I want you to drive the getaway car!" He's been a great friend since those early days.

—Ramona Jones

ROY CLARK

★★★★★

1933—

photo taken 1977

Patsy Cline
★★★

Patsy loved my cooking. She especially loved rabbit or squirrel. If you fried a rabbit and didn't call her and she found out, she wouldn't speak to you for a week. My husband Doo would go out and hunt for rabbit and possum, and I guess he would tell Patsy when he was going hunting, because everytime we'd have it, she ended up at my house. She liked the wild ones, not the kind you can go to a store and get. You can fry it just like chicken, and I would fix it for her just like that. The Thursday before she was killed, she came over after dinner to put curtains up in my house. The kids and Doo had gotten through eating, but I hadn't got the dishes off the table. Patsy went by the table, she seen the rabbit there, and she grabbed a piece of rabbit and started eating on that thing. She eat that piece and had another one 'fore she left.

—Loretta Lynn, from "You're Cookin' It Country"

I just loved Patsy, loved her as a person. She worked a lot of shows with me in her earlier days and I knew back then how great she was. She could just hit it as a singer, and there was no work to it. She just had the voice. It was there and she used it in a great way. The sad thing was she didn't really know how good a singer she was. I have a picture in my dressing room she autographed personally to me with a really nice note on it. She wrote, "If all the men in the world were like you, what a wonderful world this would be," and I thought that was a wonderful compliment. I spent a lot of time with her in the late '50s and I admired her a lot because she would always be straight out with you and tell you exactly how she felt about something. She didn't pull any punches or try to sugarcoat things. She just told you the way that it was. She was the real thing, and just a terrific person to be around.

—Porter Wagoner, told to Rob Simbeck

I was in the Army until March of 1959 and during that time Patsy got an allotment check from the government for $137.50 a month. When I got out, we wanted to come to Nashville, Patsy to sing, me because of the printing business, but we didn't have any money so we went back home to Winchester, Virginia. I got a temporary job and she was working local dates, just wanting to get to Nashville. Another allotment check came and we thought maybe because of the way they paid them it had come late, so we cashed it and spent it. Then the next month another one came and we knew that wasn't ours, so we just set it aside. For six months, they kept coming and we kept setting them aside. About that time, we were feeling pretty down and really wanted to get to Nashville. We knew we shouldn't have been getting the checks but finally we wanted to go so bad that we cashed all six and that's how we got to Nashville. Of course, the government caught up with their mistake and got ahold of us, but they were very nice and gave us a payment plan and we eventually paid it off, but we had gotten to Nashville.

—Charlie Dick

PATSY CLINE

1932—1963

photo taken 1961

Cowboy Copas

★ ★ ★

My dad spent a lot of time on the road, so he always looked forward to the days he could spend at home doing normal things. I remember one Saturday morning when he was out on his riding lawn mower in his floppy shorts, T-shirt and ball cap, and a tour bus pulled up. That was a pretty normal thing for us. Little Jimmy Dickens lived across the street, George Morgan lived down the street and Roy Acuff was a little farther down the road. The bus stopped in front of our rail fence, and quite a few people got out and starting taking pictures. Now, dad was one of the snappiest dressers in the business. One of the Opry announcers called him "the best-dressed gent from the West," and he generally wore a big white hat, tailored outfit and boots. Apparently the tourists streaming off the bus didn't figure the guy on the mower could be anything other than yard help, though, because a couple of them got dad's attention and said, "Would you mind driving over to the side so we can get a good, clear picture of Cowboy Copas's house?" He said, "Oh, sure, I don't mind at all," and he drove the tractor to the side of the yard and waited until they got their pictures and got back on the bus. We talked about that for a long time.

Dad had a real winning streak in the late '40s and early '50s when he had one hit after the other and traveled with his own band. Then, for several years, the hits stopped and he couldn't keep a band on the road, so he did solo shows and if he hadn't worked with some smart financial people it would have been really rough. Then, in 1960, he was in the studio working on a record and they finished the four songs they had planned early. They stood around for a few minutes trying to decide what else they could throw in to fill the time. Dad said, "Well, let me do one of these little songs I've been doing all my life," and they recorded a song called "Alabam'." It was the perfect example of what I call serendipitous occasions, because that afterthought became the number one hit of his lifetime, staying at the #1 position on the *Billboard* chart for 12 weeks. It was the start of a huge comeback for him, all because they had a little time left over.

—Kathy Hughes, told to Rob Simbeck

Grandpa and Copas hunted together a lot, and I remember one time they went up to Virginia to hunt with another entertainer, Joe Wheeler. They were supposed to meet him at a cabin in the mountains, and it was getting late by the time they got there. It was almost dark and they didn't know exactly where the cabin was, so they parked the car and walked into the woods to look for it. Finally it was pitch dark and they couldn't find the cabin and when they came back to the road they couldn't find the car either. They spent the night rambling around, and when they finally got back to Nashville they looked as bedraggled as two whipped mountain men.

—Ramona Jones

38   Cracker Barrel Old Country Stores

COWBOY COPAS

★★★★★

1913–1963

photo taken 1961

Jimmy Davis

I was always impressed with Jimmy, the fact that even with his humble beginnings, he had this air about him. He was the ultimate Southern gentleman. He talked the talk and walked the walk. You just got the idea he woke up every morning with a suit and tie on, like an old Southern country lawyer. That's just who he was and what he was about. I went to his 100th birthday and I was amazed at how, even at 100, he was incredibly healthy. I understand one of the reasons he stayed that way was that if he got a sniffle, he went to the doctor. He just really took care of himself. I got to see him and his wife Anna, who I remember from the Chuckwagon Gang, recording together once at the old RCA Studio. They were doing "Suppertime," which was part of my upbringing—"Come home, come home, it's suppertime." She had laid down her tracks, and I'll never forget the sight of that old man kind of hunched over that microphone, singing to her voice in his earphones. I thought, "Pinch me. Is this really happening?"

—Keith Bilbrey, told to Rob Simbeck

I had a great admiration for Jimmy Davis. I did his song "Suppertime" several times on my TV show and on the Grand Ole Opry. He was a wonderful man and a wonderful songwriter, not only for "You Are My Sunshine," which is an all-time classic, but for so many others, both country and gospel. When he sang a song like "Where The Old Red River Flows," it just rang true.

The last time I saw him was at the Opry, probably about a year before he passed away. I talked to him in the Green Room for quite a while. He was a straightforward, friendly man and he didn't really talk to a lot of people backstage. I suppose he knew that I had a lot of admiration for him, because both as a songwriter and as a politician he was the real thing.

—Porter Wagoner, told to Rob Simbeck

JIMMY DAVIS

★★★★★

1899—2000

photo taken 1979

Jimmy Dean

★ ★ ★

One summer, I spent a week on Jimmy's boat, the Big Bad John, which he had docked in Booth Bay Harbor, Maine. It was right in the harbor, downtown, and every morning we would watch these sightseeing boats that would come past us on their way out to sea. We would be eating breakfast on the rear deck, and inevitably the tour guide would say, "and on your left, ladies and gentlemen, there is Jimmy Dean and his boat, the Big Bad John," and you could see all these little old ladies leaning out with their cameras, taking pictures of Jimmy and the boat.

At that point, Jimmy would get up and stand at the back of the boat and yell, "Buy sausage! Buy sausage!"

—**Bill Anderson, told to Rob Simbeck**

Jimmy and I don't see each other very often, but it never feels like we've been apart very long at all. When we do run into each other, it starts without a word, with a handshake, a big smile, and a hug. Then we back up and see who fires the first joke. For years, I always hounded him for free certificates I could redeem for his Jimmy Dean's sausage. Even when we were on the air, I'd always say, "You're doing really well. You can afford to give me a few coupons for sausage and biscuits." Every time I'd see him I'd hit him up for them.

He'd call me a cheap so and so and we'd get a good laugh out of it. Well, one time when Lorianne and I were doing *Music City Tonight*, the staff producer told us, "Jimmy sent a surprise for you tonight." So, out rolls this miniature scale model of a Jimmy Dean Sausage semi. I was told to open the back of the truck and when I reached in it was just filled with sausage coupons. And every one of them was expired. It was just the kind of thing Jimmy would do, and I'm sure he was rocking back and forth on the couch at home laughing when he saw it.

—**Charlie Chase, told to Rob Simbeck**

JIMMY DEAN

★★★★★

1928—

photo taken 1967

Little Jimmy Dickens

★★★

"I'm not that great a singer or player," Jimmy Dickens said to me one night backstage at the Opry. "I consider myself an entertainer." Five-and-a-half decades after he'd joined the Opry, he could still delight a crowd with a mix of songs delivered in a big, brazen voice, and often self-directed jokes and stories. Backstage, he launched into one of his favorites, involving his presence at a pivotal moment in country music history. He was new to the Opry, and he was riding with Hank Williams in Minnie Pearl's plane toward a gig in Wichita, Kansas. "Tater," said Williams, using Dickens' nickname, "you need a hit, and I'm going to write you one. You got any paper?" Realizing he was being drafted into secretarial service, he borrowed paper and pen from Minnie and began writing as Williams started quoting lines. "When he finished up," Dickens said, laughing, "he had written "Hey Good Lookin'" in about 30 minutes, and he said, 'Now you take that and you record that and it'll make you a hit.'" Dickens had no doubt about its potential, but when he ran into Williams a week later, Hank said, "Tater, I recorded your song today. Too good a song for you, Tater. Too good a song." There wasn't a trace of anything but glee in Dickens' laugh as he told the story—glee that he had known Hank, had travelled with him and cut up with him. Hank's star would shine brighter, but Tater would know another half-century of turning his 4'11" frame into a joy-producing entertainment machine. And you could tell he enjoyed most all of it.

–Rob Simbeck

After his first hit record, Little Jimmy Dickens couldn't wait to travel back to the hills of West Virginia to show his Grandma and Pap his new Cadillac limousine. He got the car down the gravel road and through the woods and pulled up in front of the old house. Inside, Ma was fixin' eggs and ham and Jimmy was talking to her, when he glanced outside and saw Pap steppin' off the Cadillac to see how long it was. Jimmy went outside and Pap said, "Jim, what kind of car is she?" Well, Jimmy knew that Pap thought the only good car ever made was a Buick, so he replied, "She's a Buick, Pap." Pap just smiled, shifted the chaw of tobacco around in his mouth and said, "Wouldn't you know." Later, Jimmy took Pap to town and Pap sat in the back while Jimmy drove. Jimmy was watching Pap in the rear view mirror and noticed that Pap's chaw of tobacco was getting mighty moist as he was trying to figure out how to roll down the back windows. Finally Pap hollered, "Jimmy, how you get this window to roll down?" Jimmy answered, "Just point your finger at it," watching in the mirror as Pap pointed his finger, at which time Jimmy hit the electric window button that controls the back seat windows. Pap spit brown tobacco juice all down the side of Jimmy's new Cadillac limousine. This went on all day as they drove around the area, showing off Jimmy's new car, Pap pointing his finger at the window and Jimmy rolling it down. When Jimmy finally told him, Pap made Jimmy swear he wouldn't tell anyone because he was afraid the people in the white coats would come and pick him up.

—**Stan Hitchcock,** from *At The Corner of Music Row and Memory Lane*

"LITTLE" JIMMY DICKENS

★★★★★

1920—

photo taken 1976

Everly Brothers

★ ★ ★

From 1952 until 1956 I worked for Associated Photographers in Nashville, out near Vanderbilt University. Like many people in those days, we didn't own a car, and I relied on public transportation to get into town from Madison where we lived. I did have a friend with a car who would pick me up at the bus stop on his way into town if he came by before the bus arrived. On many of these occasions, there would already be two passengers in the car with him. Their names were Don and Phil Everly, the children of entertainers Ike and Margaret Everly. One morning that really stands out in my mind was when my friend stopped at Fourth and Deaderick Streets to let the Everlys out. I watched as they walked up the hill, presumably to WSM. They looked hopeful. One was carrying a demo recording under his arm. It was probably one of Boudleaux and Felice Bryant's songs, since the Everly Brothers recorded and made hits of many of their songs over the years. Not long after that day, those two young men went on to become a household name and were one of the first acts to cross over that now sometimes fine line between country and pop music. In 1957 they actually had 6 top ten country tunes and 7 top ten pop tunes all playing on the air at the same time. I remember Ott Devine, the Opry manager at the time, saying, "Yes, and they started on the Grand Ole Opry!"

—Les Leverett, told to Libby Leverett-Crew

When the Everly Brothers were teenagers, they used to catch a ride into town and hang out with the musicians at the Grand Ole Opry. They were really interested in the music business and in country music and you'd see them there every Saturday night, way before they got their first deal with Cadence Records. We got there for the early shows, and we'd leave around 11 and I would always ask them if they needed a ride home, because I lived not far from them. Usually they did. Well, one time around Christmas, we were headed home and Phil was sitting in the back seat and Don was in the front with me and there was a package sitting between us. He said, "Gordon, what's in the box?" and I said, "Open it up." It was a smoking jacket and I told them it was a Christmas present we had bought for Elvis. We'd had it monogrammed with an "EP" for him. We recorded with a lot of people at the time, but it was always Elvis that the Everlys were asking us about—when had we last seen him and what was our last session with him like—and so they were excited out of their minds to see that jacket. In fact, I saw Phil not long ago and he brought that day up. He said, "I will never forget that. I could not believe I was looking in the box at an Elvis Presley Christmas present." They're very special people and they've been very dear friends of ours since the beginning.

—Gordon Stoker, The Jordanaires, told to Rob Simbeck

EVERLY BROTHERS

★★★★★

Isaac Donald Everly 1937—, Phillip Everly 1939—

photo taken 1960

Flatt & Scruggs

Back in 1961, WSM loaned me to NBC television, which was doing a series called *Here And Now*, with one of their top commentators, Frank McGee. One show focused on Flatt & Scruggs, who were really coming into their own at the time and were making waves across the country. I went on two bus trips with them. One was to Cave City, Kentucky, where they entertained from the top of the concession stand at a drive-in movie theater. A few days later we went to Jumpertown, Mississippi, where they entertained in a high school auditorium for a very responsive crowd of people. It was a great time for me because it was my initiation into traveling on the road with a group of musicians, every one of whom I respected and admired. I got to witness first-hand how difficult it is to sleep on the bus while sitting up and how eating at roadside restaurants can get very old. What I learned, though, was that these guys loved their music so much they would go through whatever life on the road had to offer, over and over, just to be able to play. Those two road trips rate up at the top of my career highlights.

—Les Leverett, told to Libby Leverett-Crew

Flatt & Scruggs were what every band wanted to be. They had the complete package. Because of their affiliation with Martha White as their sponsor they were able to make enough money to keep the same band year in and year out, so they had great instrumentation. Then, Earl Scruggs was just the best banjo player there ever was. He revolutionized that instrument, and his presence today is still being felt. He's one of the greatest instrumentalists ever, not just in country music, not just in bluegrass—he is one of the single most important musicians in the world. Lester was phenomenal as a guitarist, a singer and a songwriter, but what Lester also had was that he was such a great emcee. There were people who came to see them just to hear Lester talk, because he was so believable, so natural. He was someone who came out of radio, where every second was precious and you learned how to communicate. You knew how to handle that microphone in between songs. We don't have emcees in our business anymore, and we don't have acts—showmen with as many instrumental and vocal and songwriting skills—like Flatt & Scruggs anymore.

—Eddie Stubbs, told to Rob Simbeck

FLATT & SCRUGGS

★ ★ ★ ★ ★

Lester Flatt 1914—1979, Earl Scruggs 1924—

photo taken 1965

Tennessee Ernie Ford
★ ★ ★

In 1984, President Reagan presented Ernest Jennings "Tennessee Ernie" Ford with America's highest civilian honor, the Medal of Freedom. This honor is reserved for individuals the president deems to have made commendable contributions to the security or national interests of the United States, to world peace, or to cultural or other significant public or private endeavors.

I first met "Tennessee Ernie Ford" on March 1, 1961 at the Holiday Inn behind the Tennessee State Capitol, where he, his wife and their usual entourage were staying. They had arrived a few days earlier, by train from California, to take in the sights before they played an engagement–an annual charity fundraiser at the Tennessee State Fairgrounds. It was my job to travel with him and photograph the events. While in Nashville, he visited every place imaginable. He made stops at all the local radio stations, and made guest appearances on various television shows. He stopped for a game of golf with the governor, visited several women's clubs, and toured local hospitals. There was even a marvelous reception at Richland Country Club, one of Nashville's most prominent country clubs, with quite an impressive guest list.

Ernie Ford was kind and generous and he loved to laugh–all the ingredients of a man who possessed honor, something that even a president recognized. During that eventful week, I was lucky enough to get to know Ernie. When his final night in Nashville finally arrived, several of us went down to the Union Station to see him off. Minnie Pearl and her husband Henry Cannon were there, as were Dot and I and our two young boys, John and Gary. He was turning to leave when he noticed my two little guys standing there, and asked if they were my sons. I replied, "Yes, sir." He grabbed them, knelt down between them, and waited for me to get my camera focused. That photograph of the three of them is a priceless thing and a wonderful souvenir of a fabulous week. A man of honor is a man who does more than what is expected of him–a man like Tennessee Ernie Ford.

—Les Leverett, told to Libby Leverett-Crew

Tennessee Ernie Ford studied classical music as a young man, and he brought the power and control of an opera singer to the genres where his heart and soul was—country and gospel. He also knew that both had riches the masses would come to appreciate. Toward the end of his life, he said, "I knew country music had the potential to become what it has become and I knew gospel music would be perceived as much more than sad wailing on the ash heap. Both of those things have happened just as I expected."

—Bill Littleton

TENNESSEE ERNIE FORD

★ ★ ★ ★ ★

1919—1991

photo taken 1961

Merle Haggard
★ ★ ★

I ate breakfast with Merle once at the Cracker Barrel near the Opryland Hotel, and he made two statements that have always stuck with me. One was that he believed there was such a thing as luck, and the other was that it was harder to get out of the music business than it was to get into it. He said, "When you first start out, the fans practically have to scream and roll around on the floor in the record shop and demand your record before anyone notices you. Then after you have been at it for several years, quitting is virtually impossible, because by then you have so many people depending on you for a paycheck." He was referring, of course, to the bus driver, sound and lighting people, and his band. It was an interesting perspective from one of the greatest country singers the world has ever known.

—John Riggs

Stardom can be a strange mixture of glamour and squalor, excitement and tedium. Merle once said he never charged anybody for the hour he spent on stage. He charged them for the 23 he spent riding buses and doing the rest of what's behind that brief interval. One of the best examples of stardom's split personality came when Merle and his band the Strangers were asked to play for first lady Pat Nixon's birthday party at the White House in 1973. A bedraggled and hungover Merle and his band shuffled into the White House for an event that smacked of propriety and glamour. If there's anything Merle wasn't, it was intimidated. He had just played a show with one of his heroes in the front row. "If I can play 'Faded Love' for the great Bob Wills," he said, "I can sing for President Nixon." Three songs into the set, though, things looked different. Merle was getting absolutely no reaction from Pat, the president, or the dignitaries who were taking their cues from the first couple. "There they sat, with no expressions whatsoever," Haggard said. Nonplussed, then angry, Merle addressed Pat directly, then dedicated Jimmie Rodgers' "California Blues" to President Nixon. After a moment or two, the president, a California native, nudged Pat, smiled, and applauded, which gave the rest of the audience its cue to loosen up and show their appreciation. After the concert, the president and a man who had just a year earlier been pardoned by California governor Ronald Reagan for offenses that had put him in San Quentin, were comparing their early years in the Golden State. Nixon, in fact, knew the names of all of Merle's band members, and the two had a great chat. It was a red-letter day for country music and for humanizing an enigmatic president.

—Rob Simbeck

MERLE HAGGARD

★★★★★

1937—

photo taken 1967

Tom T. Hall

★ ★ ★

There is always a story behind the "making of" an album cover. Occasionally, you are at the mercy of the circumstance and you have to test the limits of your imagination. In 1969 I was asked to shoot the cover for Tom T. Hall's upcoming album, entitled *Homecoming,* after his then-current hit. I was working a regular job and could only schedule the shoot on Labor Day. The morning of the shoot, I woke to a steady misting rain. My heart sank when the telephone rang and I heard Mercury Records representative Rory Bourke's voice on the line. He was calling to cancel the shoot. At the time, I really needed the money and didn't have any more days off, so I needed to come up with something fast or lose the job.

I said, "Wait a minute, Rory. The title song off this album is a gloomy song, and this Ektachrome film that I use takes on a bluish tint in the shadows. This song is about a son returning home to visit his dad soon after his mom had died. He was too busy to attend her funeral, and the song conveys a feeling of remorse. Let's go ahead and make the photo." He agreed, so we met at Tom's house, south of Nashville. My brain kicked in again and before we left to go in search of our location, I asked Tom if he had any black thread. He did, and came up with a whole spool. We drove around looking for a graveyard in which to take this photo and actually found one. I shot a few frames of Tom looking out over the tombstones, and one of them was used on the back of the album. But the real jewel was the cover photograph. We found an entranceway to an old estate that had columns on either side of the driveway, and we could shoot the photo without the owners noticing us. Since it was relevant to the song, I made sure that we could see Tom's Cadillac in the background, with him standing, looking down, presumably at a grave. I took the thread we had brought with us and attached it to the bottom of Tom's tie, and attached another piece to the bottom of his raincoat. I had Rory stand out of the frame and pull the thread up until it looked like they were blowing in the breeze. You could see the rain on his face. For that particular song and album title and my interpretation, I believe that this is probably one of my favorite album covers that I have done.

—Les Leverett, told to Libby Leverett-Crew

TOM T. HALL

★★★★★

1936—

photo taken 1977

Bob Hope

Bob Hope came to the Opry one time when both he and Roy Acuff were well up in years, and I was so impressed watching the two of them interact with each other. Bob went in Roy's dressing room and I'll never forget the sight of these two legends sitting there talking to each other like two old men in a barber shop. Roy would tell a country music story and Bob would come right back with something that happened in Hollywood that was similar. I just sat there and tried to soak it all in. I mean, here are two icons in their fields, men whose backgrounds and experiences were totally different and yet totally the same. Then they walked out on stage. I don't know that they'd ever worked together before, but Acuff did like he did with Minnie. He played the straight man while Bob told the jokes, and it was flawless. There was no prompter, there was no rehearsal, but it was flawless, two old pros just doing their thing for an appreciative audience. It was really something.

—Keith Bilbrey, told to Rob Simbeck

Bob Hope is easily one of the most honored entertainers in the history of show business. The awards he's received reflect his talent as a comedian, his passion for sports, particularly golf, and his untiring dedication to the men and women of the armed services. He received the Presidential Medal of Freedom and the Congressional Gold Medal. Among the many things named for him were a PGA golf tournament, the corner of Hollywood and Vine ("Bob Hope Square"), an airport, a naval vessel, an aircraft, a theater and an asteroid. He has four stars on the Hollywood Walk of fame, for motion pictures, TV, radio, and live theater, and he was named one of the best comedy acts ever in a 2005 poll among peers.

Picking a favorite among those might be a daunting task, but it wasn't for Hope. In 1997, Congress declared him an honorary U.S. veteran because of his long history of entertaining troops around the world. It was a distinction that had never been given to anyone. He said, "I've been given many awards in my lifetime, but to be numbered among the men and women I admire the most is the greatest honor I have ever received."

—Rob Simbeck

BOB HOPE

★★★★★

1903—2003

photo taken 1970

Ferlin Husky

★ ★ ★

I used to tour a lot with Ferlin, and one Saturday night we worked a show together in Panama City, Florida. On Sunday morning, we were both catching the same plane, a little DC-3, to Atlanta. Ferlin showed up impeccably dressed, as he always does, with a sport coat and nice open-collar shirt, but he looked a little rumpled himself. It was pretty obvious that he hadn't been to bed yet. In those days, the stewardess would come up and down the aisle and ask for your ticket, and by the time she got to Ferlin he was fast asleep. She kind of jostled him awake and said, "Sir, may I see your ticket?" and he reached inside his sport coat and pulled out a king-size tube of Colgate toothpaste, which he handed her before falling back to sleep. I'll never forget the look on her face, which said something like, "What am I supposed to do with this?" She shook him awake again and said, "Sir, I need to know your name." He looked at her and said, "George Morgan," and proceeded to start singing George's big hit "Candy Kisses." Then he went back to sleep and stayed that way to Atlanta.

Ferlin was always an adventure. He was a fun guy, and for good measure there wasn't an entertainer in the business who could follow him on stage in the '60s.

—Bill Anderson, told to Rob Simbeck

I saw Ferlin recently at the Opry during CMA Music Festival week, and we talked in my dressing room about driving to Iowa after a date in Wichita, Kansas. We hit Kansas City that morning during rush hour traffic and it was pretty much stopped. He would get out of the car and keep his head down and slip up beside the car in front of us, then pop up by the driver's window and go, "Boo!" I said, "It's a wonder you didn't get us killed!" He said, "That was Simon, not me," meaning his comedy alter-ego Simon Crum. Most all of the time he was in a fun mood, and he spent more time as Simon than he did as Ferlin. But when he got on stage, he was a great entertainer, one of the best I've ever seen for going out and really shaking an audience up, even in the days when he didn't have a hit.

He is also one of those guys who really carries himself well on stage. He and Roy Acuff are two of the people who, as far back as I can remember, when they walked out on stage they had that look of pride about themselves—when he walks out there, he doesn't go out all slumped over.

Anyway, he went out to perform on the 10:30 show this recent night at the Opry and he did "Dear John Letter" with Jean Shepard and it was just a magical moment.

—Porter Wagoner, told to Rob Simbeck

FERLIN HUSKY

★★★★★

1925—

photo taken 1984

Burl Ives

★ ★ ★

Burl and his manager told me about the time they were having dinner at a nice restaurant not far off Broadway. Peter Ustinov was starring in a Broadway play at the time, and a lady walked over to their table and said to Burl, "Oh, Mr. Ustinov, I think you're wonderful." Well, both Burl and Peter were big men with beards, and there was a certain resemblance, but his manager determined to set the woman right. "Madam," he said, "this is not Peter Ustinov. This is Burl Ives." Well, the lady didn't hear him at all. She just kept right on going: "Oh, Mr. Ustinov, may I please have your autograph?" The manager kept trying to set her straight and the woman kept on fawning over Burl. Finally, Burl took the napkin she was offering and asked her her name. She told him and he signed it to her, and added, "With Love, Peter Ustinov." His manager said to him, "Why did you do that? She would have been more thrilled to have Burl Ives' autograph," and Burl said, "No, she was such a fan of Peter Ustinov, I didn't want to break her heart." I thought it was a great glimpse into the man that he was able to put his own ego aside to do that for her, because there are plenty of people who wouldn't have.

—Bill Anderson, told to Rob Simbeck

American folk music in the 1940s *was* Burl Ives. Back in Hunt, Illinois, Burl was considered "lazy" because he would rather play his banjo than do farm work. Later, he dropped out of college to hobo around the country, soaking up the songs of the working people like a sponge. Eventually he took his banjo and guitar to New York City, where he found popularity with his own radio program before recording success came his way. He moved comfortably back and forth across the divisions between country and folk music, but he's best remembered now for his work as an actor. Burl's standard instruction for songwriters was, "Bring me songs that either make me laugh or make me cry—nothing in between," and that was indicative of the emotional power of both his singing and his acting.

—Bill Littleton

BURL IVES

★ ★ ★ ★ ★

1909—1995

photo taken 1970

Mahalia Jackson
★ ★ ★

I was 15 and playing in the Omega Baptist Church in Chicago with a 50-voice choir. We had a radio show every Sunday night and the place would be packed. Mahalia would sweep in with her entourage to come and hear me, and I recall her telling me, "I remember you being a snotty-nosed five-year-old boy playing the organ, and I knew then you were a star." She had this 5,000-square-foot condo and she would have me come over there. There would be all these movie stars and people like that visiting her. People loved to be around her. She was very comical. She was like a comedian, saying things with a straight face that would make people crack up. I was just a kid, and after they would talk and eat, I would go over to the piano and she would have me sing. That's how I got to play for her.

There was a big Baptist convention in town. They organized a thousand-voice choir, and she was the guest soloist. She asked me to play the organ, and I knew her songs from those evenings at her home. She would be singing, and in between lines I would do these nice little runs on the organ. The crowd loved it and I guess I was taking a little too much attention. Laughing, she would walk over and say, "Soften down, baby, the people came to hear Halie."

—Jessy Dixon, told to Rob Simbeck

I had long admired Mahalia Jackson. She was from Chicago, grew up singing in church and eventually got into the recording business. Thank the Lord she did because her voice was a blessing to the whole world. She came to the Ryman Auditorium, which was at that time the home of the Grand Ole Opry. The company asked me to attend and photograph her performance. Dot, my wife, went with me and we met up with Mahalia backstage at her dressing room. Many celebrities do not like to be photographed. Mahalia was one of them. When she saw my camera, she said "Honey, I don't look like having my picture made!" She was smiling the whole time. My reply was, "Mahalia, you ARE beautiful and any one with a soul as beautiful as yours needs to be photographed." She really smiled then and was kind enough to allow me to take a photo of her and Dot together before the show.

—Les Leverett, told to Libby Leverett-Crew

MAHALIA JACKSON

★★★★★

1911—1972

photo taken 1961

Stonewall Jackson
★ ★ ★

Early in Stonewall's career, he came down to Georgia to play a couple of shows for a friend of mine. This was before he had made any money or had much recognition, so instead of staying at a hotel or motel, he stayed at the home of the promoter, who was also the early morning disc jockey at a little local station. The disk jockey signed on at 6 a.m., so he tiptoed out early while Stonewall was still asleep, but he left the radio on in the house. So Stonewall was rousing himself around 8 a.m. and he was still half asleep and pretty groggy, when the disc jockey went into his on-air promo for the show. He was saying, "And don't forget tonight, don't miss your chance to hear the great Stonewall Jackson!" Well, Stonewall just heard the end of it, and when he heard his name he jumped up and said, "Oh, no! I'm on!" and he ran into the living room in his underwear, thinking he was being called on stage. He was awfully glad to find out he wasn't.

—Bill Anderson, told to Rob Simbeck

Stonewall is a great guy. I first met him when he rolled into Nashville in his old pickup truck. I've always considered him a real good friend. He's a real country boy, which you can tell just by listening to him. I heard him on the radio with Ralph Emery late one night talking about Nashville and at one point he said, "I had to go to the doctor a while back to have my tonsils cut off," which is just a country expression if I've ever heard one. Stonewall is still great. He's had a lot of hit records and he's good on the stage. He's the real thing.

—Porter Wagoner

Stonewall Jackson joined the Grand Ole Opry without so much as a recording contract, let alone a hit record. He had come to Nashville in 1956, saving for the trip with farm and logging jobs. Not long after his arrival, publishing legend Wesley Rose of Acuff-Rose heard one of his demos and set up an Opry audition. Jackson performed first at the Friday Night Frolics before an official Opry debut that prompted four encores.

Named after the Confederate general, Stonewall had a tough south Georgia upbringing. When he was ten, he traded a bike for a guitar and began writing songs. At 17, he joined the Navy, and it was there that his singing received the kind of attention that prompted him to think of music as a career. He signed with Columbia Records and released hits like "Life To Go" and "Waterloo," a five-week number one that established him as a star, hitting the top five on the pop charts and earning him three appearances on *American Bandstand*.

—Rob Simbeck

STONEWALL JACKSON

1932—

photo taken 1961

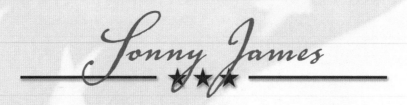

Sonny James

Three years ago I was deathly ill with complications from a rare blood disease; they literally didn't know if I was going to make it through the night. My family gathered around and they asked if there was anybody I really wanted to see—you know it's bad when they do that. Well, I really wanted to see Sonny James. As a kid growing up in Kentucky, dreaming about making a living in radio someday, I had idolized Sonny. When I first began working as a disc jockey at a local station, I used to play his stuff. When I got to Nashville and began working for WSM, it turned out that my producer, Kevin Anderson, had worked as a backup singer for Sonny. Kevin introduced us over lunch, and Sonny and his wife Doris sort of adopted me and became almost surrogate parents. Sonny was so encouraging as I tried to build my career through good times and bad, the way he was always there for so many people. When things would go wrong or I wouldn't get something I'd auditioned for, he'd say, "It's alright. Just keep moving forward. It's going to happen." He had this Andy Griffith quality about his speaking voice, just full of warmth.

I was in and out of consciousness in that hospital bed because of the medication, and I looked up one morning and there were Sonny and Doris standing at the foot of the bed. It was like two little angels had arrived, and I just sensed that everything was going to be alright. At that moment, as at so many other moments in my life, It was really wonderful to have his friendship.

—Bill Cody, told to Rob Simbeck

In the mid-1960s, a major guitar manufacturer approached Sonny, wanting to fashion a Sonny James guitar called the Southern Gentleman. Sonny agreed and a few months later the prototype was in his hands. It would have been a lucrative business decision to endorse it and let the company bring out a line of Southern Gentleman guitars, but Sonny felt the guitar just didn't have the signature sound of his Martin D-28. He explained to the company that he could not endorse the guitar, but that to thank them for their time and generosity, he would use their guitar for his posed promotional shots from then on. He was as good as his word, and the guitar appeared on some album covers and many other shots. We worked with Sonny for seven years through 1971, but few things ever impressed us more than that example of his honesty and generosity of spirit.

—The Southern Gentlemen—Gary Robble, Lin Bown and Glenn Huggins

SONNY JAMES

★★★★★

1929—

photo taken 1982

Waylon Jennings

★ ★ ★

I had the pleasure of doing a couple of Waylon album covers for RCA Records (RCA Victor in those days!). For the 1968 *Jewels* album cover, my excited 17-year-old son Gary rode along as we picked up Waylon at the RCA studios and drove to a beautiful, remote park on the outskirts of Nashville. We had a wonderful afternoon—finding just the right spot, photographing Waylon in the lush Middle Tennessee woods, watching my son blossom under Waylon's attention. Turned out we were carving a very special family memory.

For the *Just To Satisfy You* album cover, Waylon showed up for the photo session that night at my studio looking very debonair in a neat, black-trimmed gray suit. There was only one small hitch—someone had scratched the dickens out of one side of his cheek and nose! I knew better then to ask any questions but I did start to panic—I didn't have any makeup in my studio.

It's true that "necessity is the mother of invention." I decided to light his face with harsh lighting which threw a dark shadow across the side of his nose, hiding the imperfections. Turned out to be a really nice portrait. Waylon liked it and apparently RCA did too."

Right after the album came out, I saw Waylon on *The Joey Bishop Show*. Joey held up the LP and complimented the photograph. That was really rewarding. As far as I know, that was the only time one of my covers was ever shown on late-night network TV."

—Les Leverett, told to Libby Leverett-Crew

Back in 1973, I decided I would do my part to help Waylon achieve superstardom. Imagine! He had already had more than twenty Top 20 hits and had won a Grammy. Here I am a nobody making $60 a week at WSM radio and thinking I could help him do anything. I guess I just wanted to be a small part of his success when I wrote an article on him and sent it along with one of his pictures to a trade magazine. To my surprise, they printed it. I sent him a copy of the article along with a small plaque and hoped I'd get a note of thanks from him—that would make me feel good and I'd have his autograph too.

The joke was on me as I waited in vain for two or three months. Then, unexpectedly, I looked up one night and there he was coming in the back door of the station. I thought he was probably scheduled to do a live interview with the new DJ. He came up the stairs, walked into the studio, came over to me and asked if I was the one who wrote the story on him. I said, very nervously, "Uh-huh. Was it OK?" He said, "Hoss, it was great and I wanted to personally thank you." That made me feel ten feet tall.

—John Riggs

WAYLON JENNINGS

★ ★ ★ ★ ★

1937—2002

photo taken 1970

George Jones

★ ★ ★

In 1992, Frank Dycus and Kerry Kurt Phillips and I wrote a song with George Jones in mind called "I Don't Need Your Rocking Chair." I was beside myself when I got a call just a couple of days later from George! He said, "Yeah, I got this 'Rockin' Chair' song and I really like it. I think we'll cut it and kinda jazz it up a little bit." Well, this was going to be my first cut and I wanted to be there when they recorded it. I saw George the day they were recording and hinted I'd like to come to the session, but he didn't invite me. I managed to sneak in with the fiddle player, and I was actually in the control room when they were finishing one song and producer Emory Gordy Jr. said, "Hey, George, let's do that 'Rockin' Chair' song." George looked at me and back at Emory and said, "Oh, I don't know. I'm gettin' kinda hungry. I think I may be done for the day." My heart sank and Emory said, "But George, we really need to get one more. We have the band here for a while longer." George looked at me again and said, "No, I think we might oughta do that tomorrow." I was almost sick. Then he looked at me and smiled and said, "Oh, alright. I guess we can cut that 'Rockin' Chair' song." He had been messing with me! That night, I saw a dream becoming a reality right before my eyes. The band went in and recorded the track, George sang it, and it was by far one of the proudest moments of my life."

—Billy Yates, told to Rob Simbeck

There are a lot of ways to measure the importance of an entertainer in people's lives. George Jones is celebrating the 50th anniversary of his first hit, "Why Baby Why," this year, and we're releasing a three-CD box set with a hit for every year. That's a pretty extraordinary length and breadth for any career. But there's another way to gauge a person's impact. A lot of people's last request is to talk to George Jones. We get calls like that all the time, and George never turns down a request like that from someone who's dying. He will call every one of them and give them the thrill of a lifetime. And we send out a lot of signed photographs of George Jones that people are buried with. Sometimes they are people who could never even afford to go to one of his shows, but they love him that much. It's an incredible thing to witness and to be a part of.

—Susan Nadler, told to Rob Simbeck

GEORGE JONES

★★★★★

1931—

photo taken 1984

Grandpa Jones

★ ★ ★

Grandpa Jones is the only guy I've ever known who could tell you how bad he hurt and how much he had suffered and you'd stand there and laugh. He had the greatest deadpan delivery. He was talking once about his gallstone operation. That used to be a very major, very painful operation, but when you'd hear him say, "Why, them gallstones was the size of hen's eggs," you couldn't help but crack up.

—Gordon Stoker, The Jordanaires

Grandpa Jones always wanted to own a big, flashy diamond ring, but he never thought it quite fit his image. Finally, in his later years, he relented and bought himself a shiny diamond cluster set in brilliant gold. BUT...when he'd go on stage, he would take the ring, turn it around so that it would appear to the audience to be a wedding band. One night one of his fellow performers asked him a few minutes prior to the show, "How does the crowd look tonight, Grandpa?" 'Paw' stuck his head out from behind the curtain to survey the virtually empty auditorium. There were fewer than 50 people in the building. He turned back to his friend and replied sadly, "There ain't enough to turn the ring around!"

—Bill Anderson, told to Rob Simbeck

A WSM radio D.J. accompanied Grandpa from the Opry House to his car in the parking lot one night. While Grandpa was opening the trunk to put his banjo inside, a teen-age boy was parked directly behind him with the rear end of his car about 6 inches from Grandpa's leg. All of a sudden, the boy started the engine, blowing black smoke all over Grandpa's light yellow pants. This infuriated Grandpa so much he ran up to the driver's side of the car and motioned for the driver to roll down his window. When he did, Grandpa looked him in the eye and, not wanting to use any profanity but wanting to make the point, said, "Udden, udden, udden, darn you, udden, udden."

—John Riggs

When the entertainer and music collector Bradley Kincaid gave my Dad the stage name "Grandpa Jones" at the ripe old age of 22, he probably did not realize just how well the name would fit him in later years. In a modern world, this rural Kentucky native Louis Marchall (Grandpa) Jones remained a true old-timer. He knew how to make a small cut in the side of a sweet gum tree and go back the next day and collect the resin to use for chewing gum (the only kind he had as a child). He loved sitting by his fireplace, and was an expert fire builder. He knew which kind of wood burned best and which one would 'pop' too much—all of which he cut out of the woods himself. On long walks he could tell us the name of every kind of tree. Dad believed that 'spirits of turpentine' was the greatest cure for a small cut. He insisted on raising a large vegetable garden every year, even though the weeds usually took over while he was on a long fair tour. One could write a book of old sayings that he used on a daily basis. For example, he would say, "My hair looks like a stump full of grandaddy long-legs." Combine all these old-fashioned ways with Dad's quick wit, and you had an interesting character who was a real window to the past—"Everybody's Grandpa."

—Alisa Jones Wall

GRANDPA JONES

★★★★★

1913—1998

photo taken 1984

The Jordanaires

★ ★ ★

I used to do a character on *Crook & Chase* named Chelvis, who was a cross between Charlie and Elvis. I had a jump suit and fake sideburns, the whole deal. The Jordanaires were coming on the show, and Gordon Stoker, the group's legendary first tenor and manager, said they wanted to do a song with Chelvis. Gordon is my neighbor and he'd seen me do the character before and thought it would be fun. Well, there I was backstage warming up on "Teddy Bear" with Gordon and Ray Walker and Neal Matthews, three of the four who'd sung the original with Elvis in the '50s. These guys had been in the middle of the biggest entertainment phenomenon the world had ever seen. For good measure, we taped the show in a building that had once been the studio where Elvis had recorded "Heartbreak Hotel" and some of his other earliest stuff. As thrilled as I was do be doing it, just having that kind of history and vocal firepower behind me scared me. But we did it on the show, with me dressed up as Chelvis and the group singing those wonderful "bump-ba-da-das" behind me. We had fun and the crowd loved it, but I got to thinking. "Gordon," I said, "would Elvis have killed me for this?" He said, "No, he would have loved it. He had a great sense of humor and he loved hanging out with the guys and having fun." It says a lot about these guys that they're able to have fun with their history that way.

—Charlie Chase, told to Rob Simbeck

There is a rumor going around that the Jordanaires snore in harmony when they stay together in a hotel room. I don't know whether that's true or not.

—Keith Bilbrey

If there is an odds-on favorite for the act that has worked with the biggest percentage of performers in this book, it would have to be the Jordanaires. Although they may be most closely associated with Elvis Presley, the Jordanaires have recorded and/or performed live with more than 2,500 artists. Even a short list reads like a Country Music Hall of Fame, with Eddy Arnold, Patsy Cline, Jim Reeves, Dolly Parton, Roy Acuff, George Jones and Loretta Lynn just the tip of the iceberg. To date they have been installed in the Country, Rockabilly, Gospel and Vocal Group Halls of Fame.

—Rob Simbeck

THE JORDANAIRES

★ ★ ★ ★ ★

Neil Matthews 1929—2000, Gordon Stoker 1924—
Hoyt Hawkins 1927—1982, Ray Walker 1934—

photo taken 1961

Brenda Lee

★ ★ ★

An old friend of mine called one day to say he knew a young lady from California who was in town and had never seen a recording studio. He asked if I would be so kind as to show her one. I agreed to pick her up at his office in downtown Nashville and I decided to show her Woodland Studios, where I had once recorded. I really had no idea that we would get by the receptionist, much less into the studio, but it was worth a try. We walked in and I explained who we were and what we would like to do. The lady behind the desk said, "Well, Ron Chancey is producing a session on Brenda Lee right now, but I'll call and ask if he minds if you go back there." To my surprise, Ron said we could go on back to the control room.

I don't think the girl was half as excited as I was. I had loved that powerful voice in the small package the first time I heard "Rockin' Around The Christmas Tree" and "Sweet Nothin's," and when I came to Nashville, I wanted to meet her so badly, but I was sure that would never happen. We walked into the control room and Ron said, "Hello, folks, have a seat." Brenda was behind the mike on the other side of the glass partition, singing like only she can, and the musicians were playing like the professionals that only Nashville seems to attract. If this wasn't heaven, it was as close as I had been to it. When the song ended, everyone came into the control room to listen to the playback. As soon as they had heard it, the musicians said it was time for a break. That's when Brenda came straight toward us. I was so afraid she might ask us to leave. Was I ever wrong! Instead, she held out her hand and introduced herself. The young visitor was thrilled to death—even more so when Brenda took her into the main part of the studio and said, "Here, you put on those headphones and I'll put on this other pair and we'll listen to the playback together. Ron, play it again."

Brenda was a lady and a professional, and she took this total stranger by the hand and treated her like family—and, of course, earned my respect for life. After hugs and pictures, we left knowing we had been in the presence of a living American legend.

I remember telling the girl as I dropped her off just how lucky we were, and we agreed that Nashville and the music industry could never find a better spokesperson than "Little Miss Dynamite," Brenda Lee.

—John Riggs

BRENDA LEE

★ ★ ★ ★ ★

1944—

photo taken 1980

Loretta Lynn

★ ★ ★

Back in 1991, several of us traveled to play the Houston Economic Summit at the invitation of George Herbert Walker Bush. Minnie Pearl, the Gatlin Brothers, Bud Wendell and some other big executives were all aboard this chartered 727 or 737, and on the way back the pilot announced that since this was a chartered flight, normal restrictions didn't apply and if anybody wanted to visit the cockpit, they should feel free. Well, Loretta and I were the first two up there, and I've got this picture that is so cool of her sitting there with her little airline cap on. Right away, she started pointing and saying, with that wonderful country accent of hers, "What is that thing? What does that do? What's that over there?" I said to the pilot, "Could I have the P.A. mike?" and he said, "Sure." So I said, "Ladies and gentlemen, I don't want to disturb anybody, but Loretta Lynn is now flying the plane," and all the time you could hear her saying, "What does this do?" "What does that do?" And right on cue, the pilot just kind of tipped the wings real quick and you heard this big collective gasp, people taking in air all over the plane. Scared 'em to death.

—Keith Bilbrey, told to Rob Simbeck

We've done 102 sessions with Loretta over the years, and I'd have to say she's one person who hasn't changed at all. She's still the sweet, innocent person she was when we started working with her in 1962. She'd come in to a session and say, "Y'all, I'm as tard as if I'd been arnin' all day." "Well, what have you been doing?" we'd ask her. "Puttin' up poke sallet," she'd say. She was making upwards of two million dollars a year, and she was canning wild greens—just because that's who she was. Another time she said, "I guess you've never eaten my peach preserves, have you?" and we told her we hadn't. The next day she came in with a jar for everybody in the studio, but she said, "I'm tellin' you right now, I want them Mason fruit jars brought back to me," so we all emptied them into other containers when we got home and brought them back to her. Then there was the time they were filming a Crisco commercial at her house and she noticed the columns on her front porch were dirty so she went and got a paint bucket and started painting them. Two network executives came for the shoot and as they walked toward the porch she said, "Grab you a bucket around there and help me paint these columns." There's never been a thing put on about her, and people just can't help but like her.

—Gordon Stoker, The Jordanaires, told to Rob Simbeck

LORETTA LYNN

★★★★★

1934—

photo taken 1980

Barbara Mandrell

★ ★ ★

I was the afternoon DJ at WSM-AM when Barbara really started hitting, with songs like "Sleeping Single In A Double Bed" and "Crackers," that big string of hits that led to the TV series she and her sisters did. I'd be on in the afternoon, and when I played one of her records, quite often she'd call and say thanks. She'd be doing something around the house or floating in her pool and she'd call just to say she appreciated the support we were giving her. She was always like that with fans too. She is somebody who always loves and appreciates them. Anybody who would approach her to let her know they'd been touched by her music or appreciated her, she had time for them.

—Charlie Chase, told to Rob Simbeck

At a recent CMA Awards, Barbara Mandrell gave out the Entertainer of the Year award, and I couldn't help but notice that of all the women on the show, she was the one who really looked and dressed like a star. But then, she's always been that way—a credit to country music and nothing but a star.

—Gordon Stoker, the Jordanaires

I worked with Barbara from 1986-96 and it was a great job. It wasn't just that we got to play before big, enthusiastic crowds—there were pieces of history that we took part in. We got to play for the first President Bush on three different occasions, and we welcomed home troops from the first Gulf War. We got to be pretty good buddies, and I one thing that impressed me most was that she could have dinner with the president in the White House and be perfectly at home there and turn around and have lunch in a Cracker Barrel and by the end of the meal the waitresses were her girlfriends.

We were talking once and she said her favorite lunch was a baloney sandwich, and so once as we were boarding the buses at Mandrell Country to go on tour I handed her driver a card and a paper sack for her. The card said, "I wanted to treat you to lunch," and in the sack was a baloney sandwich. She told me it was one of the best lunches she'd ever had.

I also appreciated her ability to cut up. We had exaggerated country voices we'd do with each other and pet sayings. Before she'd cut an album we would go into the studio with her to cut demos of songs she liked to see what worked best. We'd be sitting in the control room listening to a playback and if one of us had done something pretty impressive—an instrumental lick or a great vocal passage—one of us would turn to the other and say, "I think you're great! Don't you?"

After ten years with her, I think she's great. Don't you?

—Dave Salyer

Barbara Mandrell

★ ★ ★ ★ ★

1948—

photo taken 1977

Roger Miller ★ ★ ★

When my father was a teenager, he worked in bands in western Oklahoma and northern Texas. He was young and green and had no idea how to break into the bigger musical world he was dreaming of. One club owner he knew had a wardrobe of flashy stage clothes and good equipment, and my father got the bright idea of breaking in and stealing it. Then, he reasoned, there'd be nothing stopping him from becoming a star. He got caught, and knew what a mistake he'd made—he would look back on it as the biggest one he ever made. Still, the club owner wrote a letter to the judge, saying he knew this kid and asked for leniency. The judge gave my father a choice—jail or the army. He chose the army, and his years in the service changed his life. He saw part of the world, learned responsibility, formed a band, and met people who introduced him to people in Nashville. It was that experience that helped form him as the man who had a real chance in the music business. When it came time to form a band and go after stardom, he went back and looked up the man he tried to steal from, and offered him a job. It was his way of saying thanks and paying a debt he figured he owed. I always thought it said a lot about his sense of honor, about his desire to do the right thing.

—Dean Miller, told to Rob Simbeck

Back in the '60s, at the height of his fame, my dad was riding his motorcycle down Sunset Blvd. At a stop light, a limousine pulled up next to him and the driver rolled down his window. "Mr. Miller," he said, "I have Elvis Presley in the back of the car and he would like to meet you." My father pulled around the corner, got off his motorcycle, and got in the back of the car with Elvis. They talked for a while, and as my dad got out of the limousine, Elvis asked my father for his autograph. It's one of my favorite stories.

—Dean Miller

ROGER MILLER

★★★★★

1936—1992

photo taken 1970

Bill Monroe

★ ★ ★

Mr. Bill's memorial service at the Ryman Auditorium drew a Who's Who of long-time legends like Ralph Stanley, Bill Anderson, Porter Wagoner, and Bill's own Bluegrass Boys, as well as younger country stars like Emmylou Harris, Vince Gill, Patty Loveless and Alison Krauss. The mood was somber, with hymns and eulogies, but toward the end of the service, my friend Marty Stuart nudged me, and he, Vince Gill, Billy Ray Cyrus and I kicked off Bill's trademark instrumental, "Rawhide." In a moment, all of us were lifted from our troubles and sorrow into the joy of the music, of his music, and we celebrated the joy that is his rich legacy to all of us.

—Ricky Skaggs, told to Rob Simbeck

In 1948, not long after my wife Dot and I met in San Antonio, Texas, she told me about meeting Bill Monroe a year or so earlier. She had been modeling in a fashion show in her hometown of Madison, Tennessee, and Roy Acuff and Bill were among the day's entertainers. When Dot came off that stage, Bill made his way over to talk to her. He said he had heard her name and seen her around WSM, and he began asking questions about her family. He was quite interested that her name was Vandiver. She thought he was a dirty old man and told him that if he wanted to know anything about her family, he could go and talk to the man with the black hair—her father, whom she pointed at as she walked away.

In 1950, we moved to Nashville, and eventually I went to work for National Life & Accident, which owned WSM. Their noontime radio show actually featured live music, and I would sometimes walk over to the studio to sit in. One day, Bill Monroe was there singing a song called "Uncle Pen," which he announced was written about his mother's brother, who taught him to play the mandolin. Uncle Pen, it turned out, was Pendleton Vandiver. I had heard that song for years, but never knew the story or Uncle Pen's last name. As soon as I got back to my studio, I called Dot and told her that I had just seen her "cousin" and told her about the connection. She laughed as she realized he was telling her the truth back at that fashion show! Bill and I became friends over the years, spending time together and even taking some trips to his hometown of Rosine, Kentucky. During his later years, we visited a few times at his home to discuss the family tree—but that day at the fashion show never got mentioned.

—Les Leverett, told to Libby Leverett-Crew

BILL MONROE

★★★★★

1911—1996

photo taken 1961

Patsy Montana

★ ★ ★

Patsy was my grandma, and when my sister and I were growing up in Mississippi, she would come from California to see us three or four times a year. She always brought her old guitar with its beat-up case covered with stickers from Yellowstone and all these other exotic places she had visited. We'd hear her play at home, and then she always arranged for a gig in Corinth to help pay for the trip. Her visits were all about music, and we considered ourselves really lucky because she also had grandkids in California—they were cousins of ours—and while they knew her as a regular grandma who would visit and cook and all that, they didn't hear her sing until she was in her 80s, when she performed at the grand opening of the Gene Autry Museum in Los Angeles. They were amazed at how talented she was and how captivated the audience was, and we got to witness that every time she visited.

What stuck with me most was how much she loved the music, and how much she valued the people who were her fans. Both of those things kept her young and kept her performing very late in life—it's hard to say exactly how long, because she had always used one-liners to avoid giving away her exact age. She would laugh and say, "I've lied about my age so long I've forgotten how old I am." She worked at her music, and she practiced her yodeling right up until her last few years. And as for the fans, even in her 70s and 80s she would hang around until she saw the very last fan who wanted to talk to her. That love of the music and the fans really showed on stage. There were others who might have been technically better, but somehow they didn't connect with the audience the same way she did. She had charisma.

—Michael Montana, told to Rob Simbeck

PATSY MONTANA

★★★★★

1908—1996

photo taken 1978

George Morgan

George was a kind and generous person that people just loved to be around. In the days when they toured in two or three cars, everybody always wanted to ride with George because he was so much fun. Part of that was being a practical joker. Once he and Jimmy Dickens decided to stage a fight backstage at the Opry. George was six-one-and-a-half, and Jimmy is a little bitty guy, but they went out into the alley behind the Ryman Auditorium and made it look so real that they actually called the police on them. Then they had this fiddle player who was jumpy and nervous, and once in a motel George spread ketchup over himself and played dead just to scare the poor guy.

I think the reason being a star never went to his head was that he was just so family oriented. He loved being a father. We had our first child, Candy, named after his hit "Candy Kisses," just 11 months after we were married and we had five altogether. He had nicknames for all the kids—he called Lorrie "Fussy" because she'd had colic as a baby—and he loved being a family man so much that stardom was second place to him. Every summer when the kids were out of school, we packed up and went to Ohio to be near his family, and every week when he flew home from the road it was like a big reunion. He'd want fried chicken and chicken & dumplings, corn on the cob and strawberry shortcake. When the kids were little, he loved to do things like point and say, "Look over there!" and while they were looking away he'd pull a bunch of candy and gum from his pockets and it would fly through the air around them. They believed it was coming from a fairy or somebody. He used to throw his change in his shaving kit, and every week when he flew back from the road one of them would get to empty it and keep the change. He was a kind and generous person, a loving husband, a great father, and a wonderful citizen to boot. Most of all, he was the star in his family and you couldn't get any bigger than that to him.

—Anastasia (Anna) Morgan Trainor

Few artists in any genre have ever had the kind of rookie year George Morgan had in 1949. His "Candy Kisses" entered the charts in February and shot to #1, where it remained for three weeks. The flip side, "Please Don't Let Me Love You," entered the charts three weeks later and peaked at #4. He would have two more double-sided hits and and another single for a total of seven major hits in his first year. For a time, he was on the tail of Eddy Arnold as a smooth country crooner, and in fact it was Arnold he replaced when he joined the Grand Ole Opry in 1948. It was a stunning debut.

—Rob Simbeck

GEORGE MORGAN

⭐⭐⭐⭐⭐

1924—1975

photo taken 1965

Willie Nelson

★ ★ ★

I do believe Willie has earned every line in that craggy face of his, and he's got great stories related to many of the hard times. He came on my morning show unexpectedly one time, and I was really glad for the stories because I certainly wasn't "on." I was coming down with a bug and I felt awful, and there was my program director, John Malone, saying, "Willie's on the way to the studio right now." Of course, I had wanted to interview Willie for a long time, but here I was unprepared and feeling awful. I was just asking what I could remember from shows I'd seen him on, and then he launched into this story, which I'd heard before and which really made for great radio. He said, "I had just gotten a divorce and had wrecked a couple of cars within a short period of time, so I didn't have any transportation." He said he was living with a friend or in his car or something. All these terrible life things had happened one after the other. He said, "I was with Hank Cochran, and we wrote, 'What Can You Do To Me Now,' and the next day my house burned down." He was telling it straight-up, not trying to make it funny or to make the song sound better. It was just the way it was. And it was pure Willie.

—Bill Cody, told to Rob Simbeck

Willie is just one of a kind. There is nobody else like him in the world. He's a wonderful man and a great friend to everyone. I found that out two years ago. I ran into him and I said, "Willie, you and I have never recorded anything together. When are we going to fix that?" He said, "I'd love to sing with you. When do you want to?" I was recording the next month and I told him a date and he said, "I'll be there. You pick the songs." I picked "Family Bible" and "When The Silver Eagle Meets The Great Speckled Bird." About an hour before the session, he pulled up in his bus and we visited for a few minutes before we went into the studio. He doesn't like to rehearse and I don't either, and we went through it one time and it was what we wanted. I tried to pay him and he said, "I won't take a nickel of your money—unless it's playing poker."

He's a brilliant guy, and I think he's got more talent than the top ten artists of today.

—Porter Wagoner, told to Rob Simbeck

WILLIE NELSON

★ ★ ★ ★ ★

1933—

photo taken 1965

Roy Orbison

★ ★ ★

I've never known a man to go through more heartache than Roy did. His wife was killed, and then his house burned down, killing his two sons. I don't know how he came through it all, but he did. He was a huge star and a great guy, and everybody loved him. We did a program with him about 11 months before he died and at one point he took me aside and said, "Gordon, do you remember the first session I did with Chet Atkins at RCA?" He told me how scared he'd been, and I remembered very well how timid and backward he seemed. This was his first major label recording experience, and he was scared to death. He reminded me that Chet had me stand just to his left and sing his part off–mike to help give him confidence and help him get through it. He said, "Believe me, I never forgot it. It meant a lot to me." This from a guy who was Elvis's favorite. Elvis absolutely loved Roy Orbison, but Roy didn't make a bigger deal out of that than he did anything else. He was really cool about everything.

—Gordon Stoker, The Jordanaires

The biggest single date Patsy worked was an outdoor show in Ozark, Alabama. She was supposed to be getting $800, but when her manager found out Roy Orbison and Bobby Vee were on the show too, he figured that since rock 'n roll paid more than country, he ought to raise her price, which he did—to $1,200. I had met Roy earlier, because when Patsy was in the hospital after her car wreck, he was in for appendicitis, and when we got to the show, he took me aside and said, "Did they tell you? Be sure you get paid before you go on." So I went to the promoter, who wrote out the check before Patsy went on and said he would cash it afterward. As soon as the show was over, he gave me $800 in cash and I said, "We were supposed to get $1,200," so he counted out four hundred dollars in one dollar bills. It looked like I had a gold mine. We hot-footed it back because Patsy had to play somewhere the next day, and not long after that I said to Roy, "I appreciate you telling me about getting the money up front." He said, "I wish you'd have told me, because I never got my money."

By the way, after that Alabama show, he went to England and somehow he lost his glasses and all he had left was his sunglasses, which he had to wear, because he couldn't see without them. People really responded to it and he wore sunglasses from then on.

—Charlie Dick, told to Rob Simbeck

ROY ORBISON

★★★★★

1936—1988

photo taken 1970

Buck Owens
★ ★ ★

Nashville may have been the center of attention for country music for most of its history, but both Texas and California have always had vital, independent-thinking artists who operated proudly outside its influence. A case in point is Buck Owens, a Bakersfield original who claimed both Texas swing king Bob Wills and outrageous rocker Little Richard as prime influences. He never masked his dislike for the smooth, polished "Nashville sound" of the early '60s.

"I didn't like the music in Nashville—soft, easy, sweet recordings, and then they pour a gallon of maple syrup over it," he said. His own recordings, done in collaboration with bandleader/guitarist/fiddler Don Rich, provided a vibrant contrast to the string-enhanced, pop-influenced sounds of Nashville. He helped spearhead a lean honky-tonk California sound which influenced scores of country entertainers as well as rockers from the Beatles to Gram Parsons. Ringo Starr, always a big fan of country music, sang "Act Naturally" on the flip side of the smash single, "Yesterday," and Creedence Clearwater Revival's John Fogerty threw the line "listening to Buck Owens" into their 1970 hit "Lookin' Out My Back Door."

By the time the hits had begun to fade in the 1970s, Owens had established himself as a TV star, co-hosting the hit series *Hee Haw* with guitar whiz Roy Clark. His red, white and blue guitar and big grin were staples of the tube until the mid-'80s. Still, by that time he had faded from the charts and his influence waned.

In the meantime, there emerged a new crop of neotraditionalists including Ricky Skaggs, John Anderson, George Strait and a Kentucky-born, West Coast-living singer with a boatload of attitude and charisma—Dwight Yoakam, who never hid his large debt to Owens. People brought Buck press clippings of Yoakam praising him and reminding fans of his importance. Yoakam asked Buck to join him in concert, and then on record, where the two went to #1 in 1988 with "Streets of Bakersfield," the first time Buck had been at the top since 1972. A year later, a duet with Ringo Starr, reprising "Act Naturally," took him high into the country charts again, and helped re-establish Buck's place as one of the true country music icons.

– Rob Simbeck

BUCK OWENS

★★★★★

1929—

Patti Page

★ ★ ★

My husband Jon was producing an album for Patti Page, and I went with him to her maple syrup farm in New Hampshire to record some vocals. We stayed at a guest house on the property, and the setting was just magical. We took moonlight snowmobile rides through the maple groves, and had incredible meals cooked by Patti's husband Jerry, who is a fabulous Italian cook. One night after a big dinner Patti and I were cleaning up the kitchen, chatting away while we worked. We fell silent for a moment, absorbed in the task at hand, Patti rinsing dishes and handing them to me so I could load them in the dishwasher. Suddenly I was aware of this lovely and ethereal sound, for all the world as sweet and pure as the voice of an angel, and I remember thinking, "My Lord, what is that?" It was nothing more and nothing less than Patti, humming absent-mindedly, the way people do sometimes when they're lost in something else. I had to stop myself and think, "Oh, yeah, this is Patti Page I'm doing dishes with!" We forget sometimes that what makes some people great is their seemingly offhand ability to take us instantly to the loveliest parts of being human. I didn't say anything; I just enjoyed the moment, and realized how special it was and how few people would know one like it.

—Kathy Mattea, told to Rob Simbeck

Patti Page was the first female crossover artist to draw country listeners into pop music, and she was a huge star in an era when great style and class were part of the package. I have always been extremely impressed with what a classy lady she is, completely diplomatic and gracious with everyone from waiters and doormen to her fellow stars. In fact, she seemed to be genuinely in awe of the fact that singers like Kathy Mattea and Emmylou Harris were working with her on a recent album, and she was so grateful for their participation. She was never sure how thoroughly country fans had embraced her, and that was especially evident when she appeared on the Grand Ole Opry. I can't think of another booking that has made her more proud.

Patti always sends me thank-you notes when I send something for her birthday or Christmas, and I have saved every one of them. I've worked with her for several years now, but I'm still a fan.

—Schatzi Hageman, told to Rob Simbeck

PATTI PAGE

★ ★ ★ ★ ★

1927—

photo taken 1970

Dolly Parton

★ ★ ★

I'd done a lot of album covers on Dolly Parton when they came up with an album called *Bubblin' Over*. She, Porter Wagoner, and her record producer, Bob Ferguson, had come up with this idea of having her leap into the air to represent bubbling over with happiness. So, I met Dolly at RCA studios, got into her big white Cadillac, went over to Centennial Park in Nashville, and found an appropriate place for her to do this "leaping." There was a little rise in the park and I shot from a very low angle so it appeared that she was leaping higher than she really was. She had on a little, tight jumpsuit, and was her usually bubbly self. The next day my wife Dot and I carried the transparencies to RCA to meet with Porter, Dolly and Bob. We went into this little conference room and projected the transparencies up on the wall. They saw what I had already seen—that little jumpsuit had clung to and accentuated a certain anatomical part of Dolly that was not appropriate for an album cover. We all knew the photo session would have to be repeated, with different clothing, and we pondered other ways of making Dolly look like she was "bubblin' over." Dot said, "Why not go over to the Country Music Hall of Fame and photograph her around their fountain?" Everyone agreed. We knew that Dolly would draw a crowd of tourists, so RCA arranged for the police to control things. Dolly stood on the edge of the pool that encircled the fountain. I took my shoes and socks off, rolled up my pants, and waded into the water in order to get a better angle. Being a mountain girl, Dolly could not resist, so I went over and held her hand while she dipped her toes in. Someone had called the local news; they filmed the session, and showed it that evening. It turned into quite an event, and the cover turned out just as everyone had imagined. I took a close-up of Dolly, and sandwiched it with a shot of the fountain. Dolly, indeed looked like she was "bubblin' over" and that cover won the *Billboard* Country Cover of the Year Award.

—Les Leverett, told to Libby Leverett-Crew

Dolly has been a great asset to my whole life, not just in music. She's a wonderful lady. When I had problems with the IRS I had to sell off a bunch of things to pay the bills, and she came to my aid. I sold her the songs I'd written while I was with Owepar music, the company she and I started. Then last year, I wanted to buy the songs back from her. I wanted my family to have them when I go on to that other Grand Ole Opry up in the sky. I wrote Dolly a letter and told her I was prepared to pay exactly what she had paid me for them, and she wrote back and said, "The songs are on the way, but I'll accept none of your money. I know how you feel about your songs because the ones I write, they're a part of me, part of my inner soul." Few people would have done that, and I told her what that meant to me. It wasn't a matter of the money. It was the personal feeling I had about it, and it shows the kind of person Dolly is.

—Porter Wagoner, told to Rob Simbeck

DOLLY PARTON

★ ★ ★ ★ ★

1946—

photo taken 1980

Minnie Pearl
★ ★ ★

One beautiful springtime Saturday, I had an appointment to go out to Minnie's house to photograph her for the Opry picture book. She lived on West Curtiswood Lane, next door to the governor's mansion. I took my daughter Libby with me that day and we had a good time. Minnie was always so cordial and sweet. She wanted me to look through her dresses for one she should wear for the photo session. We chose the dress, and then we went outside to find an appropriate place to use as a background. She had some man inside the house working on painting or carpentry, or something. Outside, there was a yard man raking, trimming, and cleaning her yard. And if that wasn't enough, there was a swimming pool service man cleaning the pool. Minnie looked around at all of these men working, and said, "There are days that I wish that I was still back in Centerville, where I didn't have to have all of these people to keep things going." She meant it to be humorous, but it came across to me as sad. She was in her own trap of success, not being able to take care of her own needs, but having to hire people to do things for her. We posed her and, in some exposures, her and her little dog, sitting near her azaleas, and on the steps going up to her garden. She looked regal, and a long way from Centerville. Minnie had a wonderful way of putting things in perspective, though. She knew that she was where she was needed. If not for all of the people taking care of things for her, she would not have had the opportunity to share her wonderful self with the world.

—Les Leverett, told to Libby Leverett-Crew

I used to do a Minnie Pearl impersonation in the Country Music USA Show at the Opryland theme park, and sometimes we would be contracted to do shows for corporate events. The first time I met Minnie was at one of those shows. I was to go out and do my impersonation, and she would come out and interrupt me, then take over. As I got started, the crowd didn't know she was coming out, but I did, and I was very nervous. I remember saying to myself, "Calm down. Go slowly. Get your timing right. She's watching!" She walked out while I was doing her, put her chin on my shoulder, and said, "How-dee!" I acted bumfuzzled and walked off, and she entertained them.

She was still backstage after the show and she walked over and said, "Chely!" I couldn't believe Minnie Pearl had said my name. She said, "I've seen you doing me. I've walked over to the show in the park and you do a really great job." I explained that she'd been a big influence on me for many years and we began a long conversation. I kept thinking, "Surely I'm keeping her. I'll bet she wants to go," but she kept talking. At one point her husband, Henry Cannon, walked over to her with his hat in his hand. She was listening to me and, without ever breaking eye contact, she touched his forearm with a touch that said, "This kid wants to be talking to me. Give me a minute," and Henry went back and sat down and picked at the threads on his hat. There was so much exchanged between those two people with that small gesture. They said Ronald Reagan was the Great Communicator, but if Minnie wasn't better, she was at least as good. I've never forgotten it.

—Chely Wright, told to Rob Simbeck

MINNIE PEARL

★ ★ ★ ★ ★

1912—1996

photo taken 1961

Carl Perkins
★ ★ ★

Carl was in the studio with me once and he was telling me how he wrote "Blue Suede Shoes." He said he was sitting out on the landing of a stairwell at the housing project in Jackson, Tennessee, where he and his wife lived. He had come in late from doing this gig where he had been watching this guy who was wearing some new suede shoes. The guy was with this beautiful girl—Carl said the man was way out of his league with her to begin with—but all he could talk about was those danged shoes: "Don't mess up my shoes," the guy kept saying to people. Carl said, "It really kind of made me mad, so I was sitting out on the landing working on this song—'One for the money, two for the show...Don't you step on my blue suede shoes.'" He said after a while his wife came out on the landing and said, "Carl, could you play a little softer? You're gonna wake the babies." He looked up and said, "OK, honey, I'll do that," and she said, "By the way, whose song is that?" "That's ours, honey," he told her, and she said, "You go ahead and write the song. I'll put the babies back to sleep later." She knew right then it was a hit. And I was struck by the passion with which he told that story so many years later. I mean he had tears in his eyes, it was such a vivid memory to him. It was hard to imagine when you were around him that he was the icon he was, because he was so ordinary, so down-to-earth, and so humble.

—Keith Bilbrey, told to Rob Simbeck

An assortment of events changed the face of rock 'n roll in the late '50s. Buddy Holly, the Big Bopper and Ritchie Valens died in a plane crash. Chuck Berry was arrested. Jerry Lee Lewis fell from grace. Elvis was drafted. One of the biggest such events, though, receives much less notice. In 1956, Carl Perkins spent four weeks at #2 on the pop charts and three weeks at #1 on the country charts with "Blue Suede Shoes," an instant rock classic. At 23, he was apparently on the way to superstardom. While traveling to New York for scheduled appearances on *The Ed Sullivan Show* and *The Perry Como Show*, he was involved in a catastrophic automobile accident that hospitalized him. Elvis covered "Blue Suede Shoes," stealing some of the song's thunder, and Perkins wasn't able to repeat his initial success. Still, he has long since been acknowledged, especially by his peers, as one of rock's primal forces. The Beatles covered three of his songs, and Paul McCartney once said, "If there were no Carl Perkins, there would be no Beatles." Artists including Rick Nelson, Bob Dylan, Eric Clapton, John Fogerty and many others cited his influence. On the country side of the ledger, he spent ten years as an integral part of Johnny Cash's road show. In both genres, he has long been acknowledged as one of the best both professionally and personally, and he was named to the Rock and Roll Hall of Fame in 1987.

—Rob Simbeck

CARL PERKINS

★ ★ ★ ★ ★

1932—1998

photo taken 1970

Webb Pierce

★ ★ ★

He was one of the flashiest singers country music has ever known. He drove a big bluish-green Cadillac with silver dollars glued to the dashboard and a set of Texas longhorns on the hood. On stage he wore those rhinestone-studded outfits made by the great tailor-to-the-stars Nudie Cohen. And everyone's heard about his guitar-shaped swimming pool.

The first time I heard Webb Pierce on the radio, he was singing "In The Jailhouse Now," and I thought to myself that he had a sound that was different than everyone else's. He had, as they say, a high roof in his mouth, and his voice was sharp as a knife.

I saw him many times with his sidekick Max Powell out on Franklin Road, heading home in his big Cadillac at the end of a long day on Music Row. Once I was at a service station and they stopped to gas up and have a Coke, but I never said more than a few words to him. My real meeting with Webb took place a year or more after that, and I'll never forget it. I had set up a recording session for my friend Larry Sullivan, who called me a few days later to tell me he thought the song they had cut was perfect for Webb. I told him he could be right and that I might be able to get it to him. So I called Webb's office, which was in his home on Curtiswood Lane, and told him about it. He invited me to bring it over and said he would be glad to listen. He played the tape and listened very closely, again and again, and I could tell he loved it. He asked me if I had written it and I told him no, that my friend had. He played it again and asked if I had the publishing rights to the song. I told him I didn't and he said, "Well, I'm puzzled. If you didn't write it or publish it, you don't get anything out of it if I record it." I told him he was wrong about that, because Larry had never had a song recorded by anyone and would be my friend forever if Webb recorded his song. Plus, I figured I would always be welcome to bring another song to Webb if he liked this one.

He stood up and walked around the room as though he couldn't believe someone would do anything without asking for monetary gain. He came back to his desk and said, "Well, I like the song just as much as I like your reasons for bringing it to me, so I'll cut it." And he did.

—John Riggs

WEBB PIERCE

★ ★ ★ ★ ★

1921—1991

photo taken 1968

Ray Price

Ray is one of the greatest singers of all time, bar none. In 1956, he introduced the sound of the 4/4 country shuffle, and he kept the fiddle and steel guitar alive in Nashville at a time when the record industry was all but abandoning those instruments. In the early days, though, it took a wake-up call to help him establish his own identity. In the early 1950s, right after Hank Williams, Ray had Hank's band, with Jerry Rivers on fiddle and Don Helms on steel guitar, backing him up on records and on the road. After Hank had been dead just a year or so, Ray and his band were playing in Grand Junction, Colorado, and this guy came up to Ray at a break and said, "I just want to thank you for keeping old Hank alive." Now, the man meant it as a compliment, and Ray Loved Hank—they were good friends—but that was like a light going off in his head. He knew at that moment he was going to have to make a change if he was ever going to make an identity for himself. That night after the show he fired the whole band, and the rest, as they say, is history.

—Eddie Stubbs, told to Rob Simbeck

I moved to Nashville right out of high school and I was staying with the late Autry Inman, who had gotten me a job here, and his wife, Mary. I was down to my last five dollars and one Sunday morning he and his wife invited me to church. When I got there, they passed the plate, and I thought about that five dollars. I thought, "What have I got to lose? Besides, it's only one more meal," and I threw that five bucks onto the plate. Then I started thumbing through the hymnal and saw the title, "Just For Today," and I thought, "That'd make a good country title," and I wrote about half of it right there in the pew. We got home and Autry and I finished it. The next day his friend Ray Price came over, liked it, and cut it not long afterward. That started a long, close friendship with him. I went to work with Ray as a bass player in the Cherokee Cowboys and was there for a lot of special moments in the studio and on the road over the years.

—Buddy Killen, told to Rob Simbeck

RAY PRICE

★ ★ ★ ★ ★

1926—

photo taken 1982

Charley Pride

★ ★ ★

In October of 1981, when I was with the Johnson Mountain Boys, we opened a big package show at Madison Square Garden. Charley Pride was the headliner that night, and before the show he came back to our dressing room to get acquainted. He wanted to sing a little, and at one point he said, "Do you know any of Bill Monroe's old songs?" We started playing things like "The Old Crossroads," "Mansions For Me," "Will You Be Loving Another Man," and "Sweetheart You Done Me Wrong," and he knew the words and sang every one of them. It was pretty impressive. Well, when he was growing up in Sledge, Mississippi, he used to listen to the Grand Ole Opry every Saturday night. His family didn't oppose that, really, but they could never understand why he liked "white people's music" so much, and the lengths he would go to hear it. When Bill Monroe did a tent show in his area in the 1940s, Charley went to see it and he was the only black person there. He says he stood in the back, just outside the tent, watching it. He loved Bill Monroe and a lot of the older music, and that love never went away. Couple that with his talent and charisma, and you can see why he became the star he is. I have never seen anyone that has the magnetism of Charley Pride. At the Opry, when he comes on, people just flock to the stage and hang on every song he sings and every word he says. He has such a tremendous rapport with an audience. It's an incredible thing to watch.

—Eddie Stubbs, told to Rob Simbeck

When I first heard a demo tape of Charley Pride singing Hank Williams songs, I knew that the guy was for real and had a good voice. I didn't realize how good until I got him in the studio at RCA and heard that voice coming through those speakers. I had booked the studio and got all the good players and we did a three-hour session, with "Snakes Crawl At Night" and "Atlantic Coastal Line." It went really well and everybody liked it. I'd play the record for people on my big speakers in my office in the RCA building, and then show them his picture. People liked it but wouldn't have anything to do with it because a black man singing country was so unusual at the time. I had given Chet Atkins first crack at it, but he hadn't done anything. Finally, I ran into him at the Coke machine at RCA and he asked me what I'd done with it. I said, "I haven't done anything. I'm thinking of pressing it up myself and putting it out." He said, "Well, I've been thinking about that and we might be passing up another Elvis Presley." He took it to a record company meeting in California and did the same thing I did—played the record and then passed around his picture. They said, "No, we want to see the guy that we just heard." "That's him," he said. They went for it and Chet came back and said, "We've got a deal," and I ended up producing 20 albums on Charley.

—Cowboy Jack Clement, told to Rob Simbeck

CHARLEY PRIDE

★ ★ ★ ★ ★

1938—

photo taken 1970

Jim Reeves

★ ★ ★

James Travis Reeves was never very fond of the hard work that was one of the constants growing up in Texas. "All my brothers and sisters had to work on the farm to make a living," his sister Vergie remembered of the brother they called "Travis," "and he never did like going into the fields. He'd pick just enough cotton to make him a good seat to sit down on under a persimmon tree and rest. My brothers were after him all the time to help, and get up and pick cotton. But that wasn't what he wanted in life."

What he wanted was music. His mother would play old hymns on her accordion and encourage him as he sang along. He later remembered following her around the house, begging her to stop her chores so they could sing together some more. He eventually traded a bushel of pears for an old Black Beauty guitar, and he'd sit in the shade and sing to help himself and his siblings to pass the time. It was a voice that inspired awe even then. A black woman working in the nearby cotton fields who heard the young Reeves commented prophetically, "Just listen to that boy sing! I tell you, that Travis has done been to heaven and stole the voice of an angel. Next thing you know, he'll be in 'Shreesport' singin' on the radio." By the age of 12, he was.

That year, though, his 19-year-old brother Alton was killed by lightning. His mother, who had been widowed when Travis was only months old, witnessed Alton's death and was so devastated she took to a sick bed for weeks. Beulah drew her youngest, Travis, closer, and increasingly depended on him for emotional support. Travis decided not to resume school that fall, but to find a job and contribute to household expenses. When she recovered, she convinced him to resume his education, and he went back to school and became a star athlete and the only child in the family to graduate from high school.

Although he was an ex-athlete who could handle himself with bullies, Jim Reeves joked that he didn't care if people called him a "mama's boy," because he was proud to be one. As his career took off and he toured the world, winning millions of fans with his romantic, one-of-a-kind voice, he would send her frequent cards and letters, which he'd write longhand. He and his wife Mary would make the long drive to Texas to see their families, sometimes spending just one night before returning. He really enjoyed being home and reconnecting with his roots, and he would invariably sing his mother's favorite song, "I'll Fly Away," and rekindle the loving relationship that had launched him on his musical journey so many years earlier.

—Larry Jordan, author, "Jim Reeves: His Untold Story"

JIM REEVES

★★★★★

1923—1964

photo taken 1961

Riders In the Sky

★ ★ ★

We had a couple of days off before a show in Denver and we spent it in Colorado Springs visiting at the home of Baxter Black, the Western poet. It was really, really cold, and the bus, which has a diesel engine, is really hard to start when it gets cold. The morning we had to go, it was 15 degrees below zero, and there was no way that thing was going to crank. The bus was sitting out in front of Baxter's house, and Woody Paul got a big shovel and started getting coals from the fireplace and throwing them under the bus engine to warm up the oil in the oil pan. "This is it," I thought. "He's going to burn the bus to the ground." Sure enough, the dead grass under the bus caught fire and I looked in where the hood was open as the flames climbed up both sides of the engine as high as the cylinder heads. I knew it was the end of the road for the bus.

But it worked. Woody climbed in and got it started and we went on our way. Then later on that same trip, the bus quit in the middle of the night in the middle of nowhere. It was brutally cold again and I thought, "We're going to freeze to death right here." Woody figured it was diesel fuel gelled in the fuel line and he rolled up a newspaper and set it on fire and ran it up and down that fuel line trying to get it warm, and finally he did.

We call him "The Bus Whisperer," because when it really looks bleak, he can figure out some way to keep us going and get us back on the road.

—**William R. Maxwell**

The thing that amazes me about the Riders is that they've done over 5000 shows and each one can still be so fresh. People will come up to me as I'm selling merchandise and tell me about something one of the guys said on stage and I know it's something he says every night but it doesn't translate to the people that way. It sounds as spontaneous as though it was the first time he'd ever said it. I think it's pretty cool that they can keep it that fresh.

—**William R. Maxwell**

RIDERS IN THE SKY

★★★★★

Woody Paul 1949—, Ranger Doug 1946—, Too Slim 1948—

photo taken 1982

Tex Ritter
★ ★ ★

My daughter Debra Jean has been working with me in the office, and recently she found a picture of Tex and me that Les Leverett made in my office. Tex was just a wonderful man, and he and I worked a lot of shows together, back to the old Ozark Jubilee days. We'd fly together out of Springfield on a Saturday night going to Pennsylvania or somewhere for a Sunday show, and I remember him going with us on the Grand Ole Opry duck hunts.

I remember too one time we flew into Philadelphia and we were going to work with the band that backed the guy who was performing with us. He picked us up at the airport in a station wagon and on the way to where we were going to play he was telling Tex about the musicians. He'd say, "I've got this wonderful drummer, and a terrific bass player and a really good guitar player," and Tex was nodding, and then he said, "and I've got a wonderful accordion player." Tex said, "Wait a minute, Buddy! There *are* no wonderful accordion players" and we all had a big laugh. I mean, can you picture Tex Ritter singing "High Noon" with an accordion player?

Tex was always very kind to everybody, and he had this snort he did after he'd say something funny that was really memorable. He was really special.

—Porter Wagoner, told to Rob Simbeck

When people ask me who my favorite was among all of the Opry stars, I invariably say, "Tex Ritter." Now that doesn't cast any dislike for the others—I just always had a place in my heart for Tex. The first time I met him was in San Antonio, at the Texas Theater, where he was putting on a show in between the movies, like they did back then. I had always wanted to meet him, and I got to shake his hand in the lobby. It was about 1948. He signed a photo for my date, and I was too bashful to ask for one for myself. I never saw the photo or my date again. In the '60s, after I had moved to Nashville, I was walking down the hall at WSM and coming toward me was Tex with the Opry manager, Ott Devine. Ott introduced me to Tex and told me the wonderful news that he was going to join the Opry cast and he needed me to photograph him. After the session, the three of us went to lunch. It was the beginning of a wonderful friendship with Tex, his wife Dorothy, and their sons, John and Tom. Fast-forward about 40 years. Sadly, Tex, Dorothy and John are gone, but I had the joy of watching Tex's grandchildren and my granddaughter play together recently at an event at the Tex Ritter Museum and Country Music Hall of Fame in Carthage, Texas. I realized that three generations of our family had known each other since that first handshake back in Texas. Now that's something!

—Les Leverett, told to Libby Leverett-Crew

TEX RITTER

★★★★★

1905—1974

photo taken 1965

Marty Robbins

★ ★ ★

During the 1970s, no Grand Ole Opry member was more popular than Marty Robbins. He was a fun-loving, happy-go-lucky character who everyone described as the man with a tear in his voice. He loved to pull practical jokes on band members and friends alike. He was not the type to laugh at anyone, but he sure enjoyed laughing with them. Life was fun to him and he lived it to the fullest.

It was during the 1970s that I was working at WSM radio with Ralph Emery. We would receive calls from almost every state in the nation, and occasionally we would receive a call from fans in the Nashville area. About every month or so, we would get a call from a man who identified himself as Hank Wilson. He would always ask for a song by Marty Robbins. I would answer him by saying something like, "Wouldn't you really rather hear Johnny Cash or Merle Haggard?" But he would say no, he would rather hear Marty Robbins. We would play this game for a few minutes, then he would start laughing, because he knew that I had caught on to the fact that it was Marty himself on the line.

Every few months he would come to the station, sit behind the piano, and play requests of his songs that were called in from the listeners. He would stay until four in the morning when Ralph's show went off the air. On one of these occasions, he turned to me and said, "Hey, Slick, I would like to rent your head." (I shave my head). I asked him what he meant, and he said that he would pay me $100 a day for four days if I would write the name of his latest recording on my head. All he wanted me to do was to be seen around the Fan Fair celebration. He said, "You'll get more publicity than I will, plus $400." I said, "If you're crazy enough to pay that, I'm crazy enough to do it." His current record was "A Man and a Train". So the next day he came to the television studio and borrowed a tube of lipstick from a lady admirer, and wrote the name of the song on my head, laughing the whole time at both of us.

The following October, right before the DJ convention, Marty asked if we could make the same deal again. I asked what the name of his new record was. He said, "Love Me", and I said, "I'm not going to put 'Love Me' on my head." He said, "Well, just put Marty Robbins and the name of my record label." I said, "All right, you've got a deal." So I did it. About a month after that I ran into Marty at a convenience store near Music Row. He asked why I hadn't been by to get my check. I told him I knew he was good for it and that sooner or later he would come to the station again. He said, "When you leave the store, come over to my office and I'll give you a check for $800." Well, I did, and he did.

Looking back, I think he was probably just trying to help a struggling songwriter make a buck. That's the kind of person he was. I feel fortunate to have known him and to be pretty certain that no one else ever rented his head as a billboard to "Mr. El Paso, Marty Robbins".

—John Riggs

MARTY ROBBINS

★★★★★

1925—1982

photo taken 1981

Kenny Rogers

★ ★ ★

In 1975, Kenny Rogers was just another faded rock star, a 37-year-old whose group The First Edition had come and gone, its last hit half a decade in the past. To an outsider, Kenny's future was by no means bright. His voice was distinctive but hardly noteworthy; his stage presence was passable, but he was no sex symbol. Still, Kenny Rogers was a survivor, a man who was experienced at landing on his feet, who knew what it took to reinvent himself.

He was also a businessman. Sure, he knew song structure and harmony, but more importantly, he knew about publicity, contracts and bottom lines. He had learned the hard way, blowing a chance at following up a million-selling solo single in 1958 because he wasn't prepared with a stage act. He paid dues for the next six years as a singing bass player in the jazz-oriented Bobby Doyle Trio, then joined The New Christy Minstrels, a nine-member folk ensemble. He tried to steer the Minstrels into a more mainstream sound, and when he couldn't, he started the First Edition, which enjoyed seven Top 40 hits between 1968 and 1970 and was run as a model business organization. When at last the group gave up the ghost several years later, Rogers knew he had to rise like the Phoenix yet again. He put all he'd been through in book form with co-writer Len Epand, and the result, *Making It With Music*, remains for my money the soberest, most helpful assessment of the business out there.

At one point during the project, Rogers, who had just signed with United Artists Records and whose first album for the label wasn't going anywhere, told Epand he would make it back to the top of the charts within a year. "If I don't," he told him, "tell the readers to disregard everything I say." One year later, the second song from his second solo album was released. It was called "Lucille," and nobody would be able to disregard a thing he said from then on. With that song, the "faded" rocker, on arguably his fourth or fifth go-round, launched one of country's most storied careers.

—**Rob Simbeck**

KENNY ROGERS

★★★★★

1938—

photo taken 1979

Roy Rogers

To date, only one person has been inducted into the Country Music Hall of Fame twice—Roy Rogers. Roy helped establish the Sons of the Pioneers as a genuinely pioneering institution in Western music long before he was known as King of the Cowboys. My only opportunity to talk to Roy came during a 1993 press conference held to promote an LP he had done with Clint Black. "A lot of your contemporaries are not as healthy as you are," I said. "Why do you think that is so?"

With no hesitation at all, Roy said, "I've always made it a point to be happy." Any time he had a problem, he said, he dealt with it immediately instead of letting it fester and turn into frustration and unhappiness—which are unhealthy conditions. Seems like a simple enough solution to the problems of everyday life, and yet a lot of people don't seem to get it. Roy Rogers got it, and he shared the resulting joy rambunctiously.

—Bill Littleton

The first time we worked with Roy Rogers was not the most memorable; we were far too scared and awestruck for that. It was another time, an episode of *Hee Haw* in the late 1980s. Roy was closing in on 80. He had played everywhere and with every kind of band. Now and again he was lucky enough to be backed by his beloved Sons of the Pioneers, the group he founded in 1933 with a passion for music that was lyric as poetry, sweeping as the western prairies, tightly rehearsed to a level no folk or country band ever dreamed of. But in these latter days he was more often than not backed by competent but ill-fitting country bands whose unsubtle electric bass and drums had none of the swingy, stringy magic of the Pioneers of his youth. So we could tell he was not particularly excited to be taping the ten zillionth performance of his career, but once we began to warm up with him the old familiar sparkle came into his eyes, and he suggested, and we ran through, song after song: "Skyball Paint," "Tumbling Tumbleweeds," "Texas Plains," and more. The years melted away from his face, his posture became straighter, his gestures more animated, his eyes twinkled and his smile grew and grew. "This is just like when Bob and Tim and I started out," he said over and over again.

That day showed us a whole other side to the man, showed us not only Roy Rogers the film star, but the young Len Slye who struggled and cajoled his two young friends to stick with it through the hard times, to believe in themselves and their music. That day Roy Rogers revealed the layer beneath the gracious, genial film star that raised a generation. He revealed the passionate musician and singer who always lay beneath that veneer. That day he, and we, traveled back in time to a day when the trappings of stardom were well in the future, and music was everything.

—Ranger Doug, Riders In The Sky

ROY ROGERS

★★★★★

1911—1998

photo taken 1979

Ricky Skaggs

There is a bit of Old Testament in Ricky Skaggs' story. He was five when his father, who drove every week from Kentucky to Michigan to work as a welder, brought back a mandolin for him one Friday night. It was one of the bright spots in a hardscrabble existence, and Ricky poured himself into learning to play. His Dad taught and encouraged him, and Ricky played and sang in church and for change in a store in nearby Blaine, Kentucky. Then, when he was just six, his parents took him to see Bill Monroe, who had single-handedly fathered bluegrass music. Monroe lifted the tiny Skaggs up onto the stage, handed his mandolin to the boy and let him play. "It felt like an anointing," Skaggs said 40 years later of a moment that also launched a lifelong friendship.

A virtuoso with a calling, Skaggs blazed a trail through bluegrass music. At 15, he was working with Ralph Stanley, and he went on to stints with J.D. Crowe & the New South, Boone Creek, and Emmylou Harris's Hot Band. He formed his own band in the late '70s and, at the age of 25, hit the country charts for the first time as a solo artist. He would hit the #1 spot 11 times in the '80s, with songs like "Crying My Heart Out Over You," "Heartbroke," "Highway 40 Blues," "Uncle Pen" and "Country Boy" showcasing both terrific vocals and his often astounding instrumental skills. The string of hits would turn him into a superstar, and he would be widely acknowledged as one of a handful of neotraditionalists who helped revamp country music after the *Urban Cowboy* years. Chet Atkins, in fact, credited him with "single-handedly" saving country music.

But then, in the early '90s, his career slowed down. Career and personal problems led him to reassess his life, and he found himself turning to the one thing that still provided untarnished joy—bluegrass music. "I had made a commitment to Mr. Monroe many years before that I would do my part to keep his name and his music alive," he said, "and it was time to live up fully to that commitment. I threw everything I had into those bluegrass dates..." The response, from audience and critics alike, has been phenomenal. Skaggs has helped bring bluegrass back to dizzying heights as he has packed venues and collected awards. His mix of passion, calling, and experience has made the boyhood virtuoso into a musical statesman, a man who is one of the driving forces in a seminal American art form.

—Rob Simbeck

Ricky Skaggs

★★★★★

1954—

photo taken 1981

Connie Smith

★ ✦ ★

Connie has such charisma. She is, of course, a beautiful woman, inside and out. I've never seen one ounce of ego or unpleasantness about her, which is rare. I mean, everybody has a bad day now and then, but I've never seen Connie Smith have one. If she does, you don't know about it. She's got a great smile and laugh, and then there's that wonderful, full-throated voice of hers. I remember once TNN sent me up to Kentucky to cover Patty Loveless Day, and Patty's brother called and said, "Are you driving up by yourself?" I said I was and he said, "Would you mind if Connie Smith rode along?" I ain't stupid, and I said, "Well, sure." We were on the road a couple of days, and I had just gotten this new Ray Price CD. I put it in and she would sing along with it. Now, if you can imagine Ray Price and Connie Smith doing duets—it was really something. And back when I first started as an announcer at the Opry, every announcer had an initiation. I'll never forget I had a dog food commercial and all these artists gathered around me and barked like dogs. Tops among them was Connie Smith and her chihuahua. She does a great chihuahua.

—Keith Bilbrey, told to Rob Simbeck

June 24, 1970, was a big day for my family. Momma's favorite singer, Connie Smith, was booked to come to our town and sing at the Choctaw Indian Fair. One of the albums that we had of Connie's was "Miss Smith Goes to Nashville." I stared at her picture on that album cover so much that I memorized every detail about her. I thought she was the prettiest girl I'd ever seen. She looked like an angel.

The day of her concert I had Momma take me into town to Seward's Department Store. I picked out a yellow shirt to wear to the fair, hoping it would make me stand out in the crowd enough for Connie Smith to notice me.

After the show, my sister and I got our picture made with Connie. I talked to her musicians, watched her sign autographs for the fans, and waited for her to notice me. She never did. In a last-ditch attempt for recognition, I borrowed my Momma's camera and went to the car where Connie was sitting to ask if I could take her picture. She said yes. As it turns out, it was the first photograph I'd ever taken. On the way home I told momma I was going to marry that girl. I did—on July 8, 1997.

—Marty Stuart, reprinted with permission from *Pilgrims—Sinners, Saints, and Prophets*

CONNIE SMITH

★★★★★

1941—

photo taken 1965

Hank Snow
★ ★ ★

In my early days as a Nashville songwriter, there were two singers I wanted more than anyone else to record my songs—George Jones and Hank Snow. I was sure I would never be fortunate enough to have either put their voices on something I wrote, but the joke was on me because George was the first major act to record one of my songs.

Hank seemed harder for me to approach. Many times I would be standing on lower Broadway in Nashville and he would walk right by me, but I knew the unwritten etiquette was that until everybody knows you're a songwriter, you're expected not to bother the artists. I felt that if I mentioned a song to Hank, it would scare him off, so all I would do is say, "Hello, Hank," and he would say hello and just keep on walking.

Then one day I decided to write two songs especially for him. When I worked up the nerve, I called his office and asked if I could send a demo tape to him. I remember that his secretary was very nice, and she put Hank on the phone. I explained who I was, that I had had a few songs recorded, and that I had a couple I would like to send to him. I was somewhat startled when he said, "I'd be happy to listen to them," and I mailed them that same day. About two weeks later the phone rang and the voice said, "John, this is Hank Snow. I received those two songs and listened to them very carefully, and I'm definitely going to record one of them if you don't mind." I was thrilled, but I was also worried that his producer might not like it and wouldn't let him record it, so I asked him about that possibility. "I'll still record it," he said.

A few days later he called me to tell me he was recording it, and a little later he called to ask if I would like to come to his Rainbow Ranch to hear it. You better know I went. I knew Hank was a railroad enthusiast, so I took a pair of bookends made out of steel rail as a gift when I drove to see him. Hank told his secretary to hold all calls, because he had reserved this time for me, and he played his recording of my song, which I loved. Then he said, "You know, I knew you wrote songs, and I always wondered why you never offered to show me one." For five years, he had been under the impression that I didn't like him or his records! He never knew that the first radio hero I ever had was the Singing Ranger, Hank Snow.

—**John Riggs**

HANK SNOW

★★★★★

1914—1999

photo taken 1983

Sons of the Pioneers
★ ★ ★

I met Bob Nolan only a couple of times, but I had sung or whistled or hummed his songs forever. He was in many of the Saturday afternoon movies that I saw while growing up in the small towns that dot the plains of Texas, and he was a hero to me. Though his personal life varied from that of a movie star to a recluse, from a beach bum and saloon brawler to that of a phenomenal poet and singer, for a long time his songs were on radio every time you turned it on. "Cool Water" and "Tumbling Tumbleweeds" were heard by more people around the world than the songs of most of today's idols. He wrote "Cool Water" when he was still a college student at the University of Arizona. It was first a poem printed in the college newspaper. Later, Bob dropped out of college and literally "rode the rods" as a vagrant. He ended up a beach bum, he told me just a few months before his death.

One day he saw a classified advertisement in the newspaper for a singer. He recalled how he'd gone barefoot so long his shoes hurt his feet. So, he took them off and trained up to the Hollywood area. But his 1930-31 audition for a small trio headed by a man named Leonard Slye was successful.

Slye, of course, wasn't long for the trio. When Gene Autry went on strike for higher pay, a movie studio changed Slye's name to Dick Weston and then to Roy Rogers, and he became a western movie great. The original trio was, however, Bob Nolan, Leonard Slye, and Tim Spencer. It wasn't long before they changed their name to the Sons of the Pioneers and eventually were appearing in movies with Western star Charles Starrett. Later, the group was a mainstay for movies featuring Roy Rogers.

Tim Spencer once told me that he and Bob Nolan would learn that a movie was scheduled to start shooting on a following Sunday. He and Nolan would sit down on a Thursday and write eight or more songs for the movie. And the Sons of the Pioneers would act in the movie and sing the songs.

—Claude Hall

I met the original Sons of the Pioneers when Roy Rogers was with them. I had just started in the business and was at WRVA in Richmond, Virginia. I had listened to them growing up in Indiana and just loved their harmonies. I heard they were going to come to Richmond to play the big theater, and they called the station and asked if they could be on the morning show to advertise their evening performance. I was 18 or so and I was just thrilled to death. I couldn't wait until they got there and I couldn't wait to see their instruments, which sounded so good I knew they must just sparkle. Then when they got there they had the most beat-up old cases, and their instruments were good ones but they were all scratched and beat up, like they would be if you'd taken them around the world and played thousands of shows. But I was naive and I was just shocked at how they looked.

—Ramona Jones

SONS OF THE PIONEERS

★★★★★

Roy Lanham 1923—1991, Billy Armstrong 1930—,
Lloyd Perryman 1917—1977, Dale Warren 1925—, Luther Nallie 1935—

photo taken 1973

Stringbean

★ ★ ★

I first met Stringbean in 1954, at the Shrine Mosque in Springfield, Missouri, on a package show with Carl Smith and Little Jimmy Dickens. In later years we worked a lot of shows together, and one tour in particular sticks out in my memory.

Traveling through the Eastern States, Stringbean asked me to drive his car so Estelle could stay home and tend to her garden. I gladly agreed.

Well, in Salisbury, Maryland I started feeling bad, and by that night I had a raging fever. I'd come down with a bad case of the Asian Flu. There wasn't much to do but keep going—we had shows to do and I was the only one who could drive. This went on for two days, and two more shows, and I was getting dehydrated and weak from the fever and not being able to hold anything down, not even water.

String and I were in the middle of the West Virginia mountains when we rounded a curve and saw a flat bed truck full of watermelons. String held his hand up and said, "Chief, if you'll pull 'er over by that truck full of watermelons I'll show you how to get rid of that old Asian Flu bug." I pulled over and String bought the biggest watermelon that the fellow had on the truck, got me out of the car, set me up under a shade tree, cut the melon with his pocket knife and proceeded to stuff every bit of that watermelon down me... I mean I about had watermelon coming out my ears. But, by golly, it worked! My fever broke and the liquid from the melon just worked its magic.

Two hours later I was feeling like a human being once more. String claimed it was an old mountain cure-all and I still swear by it today.

I've thought 'bout bottling it and getting a horse and wagon and going around the country selling it for flu healer.....I could make a million.

—**Stan Hitchcock**, from *At The Corner of Music Row and Memory Lane*

Stringbean's wife Estelle told me they met at a little restaurant called Peaches, right across the street from the front of the Grand Ole Opry. She was the waitress there. They both liked to fish but when they started courting, neither one had a car—Stringbean never drove in his life—so they would get on a city bus with their fishing poles, tackle, and a sandwich for lunch. They'd go out to Radnor Lake out west of Nashville and fish all day, and then they'd get back on the bus with their fishing poles and a string of fish and come back into Nashville.

—**Ramona Jones**

David "Stringbean" Akemon

★★★★★

1914—1973

photo taken 1965

Marty and I go way back. I cannot tell you the exact year that he just dropped out of a tour bus into my life, but it seemed that once he was there, he was there. He was like a brother that blended into our family tree of friends. In the early days, when we were both teenagers, we usually ran into each other backstage at the Grand Ole Opry, or at Grandpa Jones' house. Grandpa's daughter, Alisa, and I were best pals and they held many social events, all of which involved a lot of music and dancing. Marty was one of the musicians that would play a while, then dance a while, and no matter what he was doing, he did it with a joyful, loud, "little boy" laugh. His laughter creates a chain reaction. If Marty is laughing, everyone is laughing. As we got older, Marty's solo career took off, and I studied photography. One of my instructors informed us that we had to bring a model in to our next class. I ran into Marty at the Opry the following weekend and asked if he could help me out. You should have seen the faces on my classmates, and even more, my instructor, when I showed up with Marty, his big hair, tight jeans and boots. He was wonderful. He changed expressions like a chameleon, and the silly poses...well, let's just say, he knows never to cross me. I'd hate for those shots to get out to the general public. I don't see Marty as much as we did when we were younger, before our lives as adults became so hectic. When we do see each other, we always start up a conversation about some funny event from our past, and he goes into that laugh, and next thing you know, the world is laughing with us.

—**Libby Leverett·Crew**

Marty and my son Mark met at the Opry when they were teenagers and they're friends to this day. Some time after they met we moved to Mountain View, Arkansas, and Marty would come down and visit us often. One time when he came he said he was going to make us some Hillbilly Chili, from a recipe I believe he had gotten from Johnny Cash. He bought the ingredients on his way into town and put it all into this big stock pot. When he got done it was so hot with chili peppers that it could not be eaten. He said to me, "What can I do?" I said, "I don't know, unless you add more of the other ingredients and make more of it." So he got more meat and more tomato sauce and by the time he got it to where you could eat it there was enough to feed the entire population of Mountain View.

—**Ramona Jones**

MARTY STUART

★ ★ ★ ★ ★

1958—

photo taken 1977

When Mel Tillis had his theater in Branson, everybody knew him. People were always asking for his autograph—he was a stuttering Elvis. Mel loved it, but he also loved getting away for some fishing and he loved family time. Once I was there when all his kids—Carrie, Connie, Cindy, Pam, and Mel Jr.—were there, and even his ex-wife Doris, 18 years after the divorce, was there. Mel rented a houseboat and told all of us to meet him at Table Rock Lake, this beautiful lake near Branson, for a picnic. We showed up, and there were coolers and bags full of we-didn't-know-what, and we took off across the lake. Well, Mel finds this little inlet and pulls the boat up to the shore and the family gets out. So everybody is playing and walking on the shore and Mel starts a fire and pulls out the biggest cast iron frying pan I've ever seen. I don't know where he got it, but it was huge. Now, Mel was a cook and baker in the Air Force, and he's legendary, among other things, for his cooking. He pours oil in the pan and goes into those coolers and starts pulling out bags of filleted fish he'd caught a day or two earlier. He starts frying fish and hoe cakes and cutting up onions you could hide behind and he started piling it up and as fast as we could eat it he could make it. There was an absolute mound of food and to this day it's the best fish I've ever eaten in my life. There were people going by, and I'm sure we looked like just another Branson family out on a picnic, and they had no idea it was Mel and Pam Tillis and the rest of the family cooking and eating on that gorgeous lake.

—Bob DiPiero, told to Rob Simbeck

One time Mel and Grandpa and Billy Grammer, the great guitarist and Opry member, were on tour together and they were looking for this little town where they were booked. They were having trouble finding it, and at one point Mel said, "We'd better stick together, 'cause it's gonna take all three of us to find the place. Grandpa can't hear, Billy can't see, and I can't talk."

—Ramona Jones

Glenn Sutton tells the story of the time he was staying in a house with a bunch of other starving writers, singers and musicians, including Mel Tillis, and between them they didn't have enough money to buy food. Mel was standing at the window looking out at the back yard when he spotted the neighbor's pet rabbit hopping through their yard. Mel ran out the back door, picked up a rock, and with one throw, got the rabbit, took it in the house, cleaned it, added an onion and a couple of potatoes .....and the boys all had rabbit stew.

When Sutton told me this story, I was aghast, "Y'all killed the little pet rabbit? Don't you feel guilt?" Sutton replied, "Hell, don't blame me.....I didn't kill it...Mel did...I just ate it. I was hungry." Makes me wonder what would have happened if the neighbors' cat had run across their yard instead of the rabbit....well, a hungry stomach knows no shame.

—Stan Hitchcock, from *At The Corner of Music Row and Memory Lane*

MEL TILLIS

★★★★★

1932—

photo taken 1970

Merle Travis

★ ★ ★

In the mid-'40s, Capitol Records artist/executive Cliffie Stone asked Merle to write some folk songs to compete with Burl Ives' enormously popular records. "You don't write folk songs," Merle countered. "They come about from being passed down generation after generation." "Well, write some songs that sound like folk songs," Cliffie said. Among the songs Merle delivered were "Dark As A Dungeon" and "Sixteen Tons." Rarely have songs touched the core of folk traditions as profoundly, and now they are being passed down from generation to generation.

—Bill Littleton

Back in the '60s, I was Merle's road manager for about a year and a half, driving him to dates and handling some of the business that went with touring. What struck me most about Merle was that there was a part of him that just couldn't deal with how good he was or how much people idolized him. His picking style had revolutionized guitar playing, and he had written pure classics like "Sixteen Tons," but there were times when he didn't seem to have any confidence in himself at all. I used to love to hear him play but it was all I could do sometimes just to get him to take the guitar out of the case. We'd be driving along and I'd want to hear him and I'd say, "Merle, play something, would you?" He'd say "No," and so I'd use the only leverage I had, which was the fact that he had bad ulcers. Merle needed to drink milk regularly, so we'd stop in little towns and he'd pick some up. When I wanted him to play, I'd just roar through some town and he'd say, "We've got to go back so I can get some milk." "As soon as you get that guitar out and let me hear some 'Walking The Strings' we can start back," I'd tell him. That usually worked.

Once we were at breakfast in a little diner outside of Nashville with Chet Atkins and Archie Campbell, and Chet started telling Merle just how much he'd meant to him as a role model. "Everything I have because of my guitar playing I owe to you," Chet said at one point, and Merle just didn't know how to deal with it. Chet obviously had great admiration and affection for him, and it was almost overwhelming to Merle. He turned red and stammered and just changed the subject. So I was really happy when in 1977 he was inducted into the Country Music Hall of Fame and he seemed to accept it without a lot of self-doubt, because he certainly deserved it.

—Bob Kingsley, told to Rob Simbeck

When Merle moved to California, some people were saying that he'd gotten to thinking he was better than anybody else. Well, we had known him for a long time and we knew that wasn't true. One time we flew out for a recording session with the Brown's Ferry Four, which was Merle and Grandpa and the Delmore Brothers, and Merle met us at the airport in Los Angeles. It was about midnight and we stopped to get something to eat, and Merle ordered pancakes, cut them up and poured his milk over them. Then we went to his home in Van Nuys and the next day when it got close to suppertime he said, "I've got some chickens out back. I'll kill one and fry it up for y'all for supper," which is just what he did. I remember thinking, "I don't believe Merle has changed too much."

—Ramona Jones

MERLE TRAVIS

★★★★★

1917—1983

photo taken 1979

Ernest Tubb
★ ★ ★

This particular tour, with Ernest and the Troubadours, was to be quite a treat, and it's one I will never forget. I had been invited by Don Mills, the drummer in the group, to ride along on Tubb's bus for the duration of the tour. Now, everyone knew that Tubb's tour bus was the home of an Endless Poker Game for the entire time they were out on tour, and the guys in the band loved to get fresh meat, new players like me that they could strip a few dollars off of, and help to pass endless miles of highway that was the life of the traveling picker. Well, they had the perfect victim for their poker cleaning in me, 'cause I can't gamble worth a darn.

One night, after a show in Findlay, Ohio, we were motoring down the interstate hitting about 78 miles per hour, and had a big game going, with Ernest being the big winner. We were sitting around the table, with Ernest on my left and the bulkhead and the window of the bus on my right, and there was about $300 in the pot laying in the center of the table, with Ernest raising and looking like he was going to take it all again. It came around to me and I folded, and it passed to Ernest to make his bet.....well, I noticed it was getting kinda warm in the bus, and losing my little dab of money was making it even warmer, so I reached over and sorta slid that big window open about six inches........and I learned a very important lesson......you don't open the windows on those big tour buses when they are barreling down the highway at 78 mph because the window immediately becomes a vacuum cleaner and sucks whatever is loose right out the window......in this case, the $300 in the pot that Ernest had just won. It was a moment frozen in time in my memory.,......the tens and twenties sailing right by my nose and out the window like butterflies heading for sweet nectar on a warm spring morning. After the last bill had zipped by, and I sat, paralyzed by the horror of what had occurred, Ernest, without even looking up from his cards, said, in that quiet, deep voice, "Son, you want to close that window?"

Well, that is a good example of the character of Ernest Tubb. He had a kindness and patience that is legendary, and a love for this Country Music business that knew no bounds. He was the happiest when he was on tour, in touch with his fans, living with his band and traveling to do 300 shows a year......year after year. Yes, he was patient and he loved those boys in the band.

—**Stan Hitchcock,** from *At The Corner of Music Row and Memory Lane*

ERNEST TUBB

★ ★ ★ ★ ★

1914—1984

photo taken 1968

Conway Twitty

Of all the awards Conway Twitty received, surely the one that surprised him most was his *Music City News* Award for a Nashville Network special called *On The Mississippi*. Standing backstage, a visibly moved Conway said, "I never dreamed of anything big happening for me on television. In fact, I have stayed away from television, especially where you sing a song and then sit down and talk. Well, people who like your singing might not like what you have to say, so I would rather not run that risk. I've always let my music talk for me."

And *how* it talked! After several years of rock hits following the breakthrough success of his chart-topping "It's Only Make Believe," Conway turned to country music, where he earned an unprecedented 40 #1 *Billboard* singles. The man who took his stage name from the towns of Conway, Arkansas, and Twitty, Texas, followed a simple formula for success: Determine who you are and what you do best, understand how that relates to the times in general, and then *do* it. Conway did it, and it's no wonder people called him "the best friend a song ever had."

—**Bill Littelton**

I got a call from two English DJ friends of mine who had been visiting Nashville. They told me they had been to the Grand Ole Opry, taken bus tours of the stars' homes and met several country music entertainers. I asked if there was anything else they'd like to do or anyone they'd like to meet and they asked if it were possible to meet Conway Twitty. They were leaving the next day so I told them I doubted it would be possible but that I'd try. I called Conway's business manager Hugh Carden, whom I had never met, and explained that I worked at WSM radio and that Conway had recorded some of my songs. I explained the DJ's situation and their request. He told me Conway was flying into town that afternoon and that after he picked him up from the airport, if he wasn't too tired, he might see them for just a few minutes at his office in Hendersonville. "But don't be surprised if it's only a few minutes," he said. Well, a tired but cordial Conway spent more than an hour being interviewed by them. He let them take pictures of him and his office, and he gave them each a copy of his new single and one each of every single and album he'd recorded which they didn't have. When we got in the car, they both commented, "Well, I guess you know whose records we'll play when we get back to England." The story speaks volumes about one of the kindest, most thoughtful gentlemen in country music."

—**John Riggs**

CONWAY TWITTY

★★★★★

1933—1993

photo taken 1972

Porter Wagoner

★ ★ ★

To this day, I love to watch those old Porter Wagoner TV shows. When I was a kid, I was like a friend of mine from Kentucky, who said, "I would never have gotten picked for the sandlot baseball games on Saturday afternoon because at 4:30 I'm out of here. Porter Wagoner's coming on." And I don't think Porter's ever really gotten the credit he deserved for helping bring country music into the television age, although I think getting inducted into the Country Music Hall of Fame really helped.

Porter was the first artist I ever introduced on the Grand Ole Opry, and I remember I was scared to death. But then, when it was over, I told somebody, "You know, I will forever for the rest of my life be grateful to that man. He was so nice to me."

Now, that doesn't mean he didn't go along with all the jokes. He rolled my britches leg up, and the first time I did a dog food commercial, which we did live on the air, he led everybody in gathering around me to bark like dogs. He did all that, but he made me feel like, "Hey, you're OK. You're part of us." He was very nice and very helpful, and he and I have just been great friends ever since. To this day, he's very down-to-earth. He's not forgotten his Missouri roots, that's for sure.

—Keith Bilbrey, told to Rob Simbeck

Porter and his record producer Bob Ferguson were wonderful at thinking up ideas for album covers, and they got me involved in most of them. Some of them were impossible to accomplish, but one was a pretty good idea since it won a Grammy for me in 1967 for Best Album Cover. This was a major accomplishment for me. It was also one of the most fun photo sessions I have had.

Porter had a hit with a song called, "Skid Row Joe." RCA wanted to do an album of recitations, so, they entitled this record, *Confessions of a Broken Man*. Porter dressed up in some old clothes that Bob had picked up at Goodwill and wore torn and stained old shoes that he had maybe worn while cutting his yard. Bob brushed white through Porter's hair to age him, and did his make-up, darkening the lines in Porter's face to make him look drawn. We sat him on the back steps of the Ryman Auditorium for the photo shoot and I have to say that he was very convincing. He just looked pitiful.

Porter stayed dressed in that shaggy outfit and went into an office or two on Music Row, asking for a hand-out and was rejected!

—Les Leverett, told to Libby Leverett-Crew

PORTER WAGONER

★ ★ ★ ★ ★

1927—

photo taken 1974

Doc Watson

★ ★ ★

My relationship with Doc goes back to the days when we were planning the first MerleFest 19 years ago. With his blindness and my lack of musical ability, we often joked that as we visited other festivals before starting MerleFest, I was his eyes and he was my ears. He taught me how to differentiate the various kinds of traditional music, how to listen for the different instrumental breaks, and so much more. And I was always amazed at how well his other senses were developed. We'd be riding down the road and he'd say, "Your left rear tire is a little low on air" and when I checked, it would be. On another occasion, he said, "It sounds to me like the #4 plug is not hitting exactly right. I think you need a tune-up." Next time I went to the service station, I said, "I want to know about my spark plugs" and, sure enough, the #4 cylinder plug was fouled. His favorite place to stop on road trips would be Cracker Barrel, especially if we were going toward Nashville. I remember being in one once and Doc listening to the din of conversation around us, then saying to someone behind me, "I'd recognize that voice anywhere. George, how are you doing, Partner?" and it was George Jones. When we left, he would always get a case of GooGoo Clusters as a late-night snack for himself and to hand out as treats. It's just part of him. He's a wonderful man with very strong faith that has carried him through a lot, and he's been a big influence on me, almost like a father or a coach, in ways that range from musical to spiritual.

—Frederick "B" Townes, MerleFest founder, told to Rob Simbeck

Joe Wilson, now head of the National Council for the Traditional Arts, told me about picking green beans to earn money in the summer of 1952 outside Boone, North Carolina. One day he caught a ride into town with the farmer so he could spend some of his money. He had a total of 75 cents, and the farmer charged him 25 cents each way, which left Joe with one solitary hard-earned quarter. He came upon Doc Watson, who often played guitar on the streets for tip money. Doc launched into the old fiddle tune, "Ragtime Annie," and Joe was amazed at how good he was. Doc had honed his skills working in a square dance band, playing the fiddle parts note for note on his guitar. He was so impressive that Joe decided to give Doc his only spending money. After listening a little longer, Joe was awed and couldn't resist—he gave Doc his last quarter and hitchhiked home.

—David Holt

DOC WATSON

★ ★ ★ ★ ★

1923—

photo taken 2002

Kitty Wells
★ ★ ★

Kitty Wells cut eight sides for RCA, but they weren't promoted well and she was quietly dropped from the label. She had been working as the featured female vocalist with the Johnnie and Jack Show. In January of 1952, when Johnnie and Jack came back to the Grand Ole Opry, Kitty decided to go into musical retirement and focus on being a housewife and mother. One night just a few months later, though, Paul Cohen, the A&R manager for Decca Records, approached her husband Johnnie Wright at the Ernest Tubb Record Shop, where Johnnie & Jack were hosting the Midnight Jamboree. He said he had gotten ahold of an answer song to the hit, "Wild Side Of Life," called "It Wasn't God Who Made Honky Tonk Angels." He wanted to know if Kitty would be interested in recording it. Johnnie talked to her and they listened to the demo, and she said, "I guess we can do it. If nothing else, we'll get a union session fee out of it." As most people know, that record became the first #1 hit ever for a female country artist, and her retirement was rather short-lived.

Although she doesn't wear it on her sleeve, Kitty is a very religious person, and yet many of Kitty's songs dealt with being abused or cheated on or dealing with a drinking husband. I asked her if that ever bothered her to sing those types of songs because they were such a contrast to her own lifestyle. She said, "No, because I like those kinds of songs, and I know a lot of other people who like them. I don't have a problem singing in dance halls or other places where alcohol is served. I don't believe you have to live the lifestyle in those songs in order to be able to sing them." To this day when you're in the presence of Kitty Wells, you're in the presence of greatness. She radiates poise, professionalism, dignity, and class, on stage and offstage. She went on to become acknowledged as the Queen of Country Music, and it's a title that, for my money, she'll always hold.

—Eddie Stubbs, told to Rob Simbeck

KITTY WELLS

★★★★★

1919—

photo taken 1976

Dottie West
★ ★ ★

I had been asked if I would appear at a concert on the Grand Ole Opry stage, and I was thrilled because not many gospel singers are extended that invitation. During the coming weeks, it was changed to a country/gospel TV show, and I was getting more excited by the day. Finally, they called to say there had been a change of plans, and my heart dropped. The speaker went on, but I could only think about having passed up an opportunity to go to California to appear on TV with Dolly Parton. I was only half-listening until I heard the words "Dottie West," and I said, "Will you repeat that?" "Jessy," he said, "will you serve as co-host of this TV show with Dottie West?" I had the same feeling I had when Paul Simon had said he wanted to work with me—I was dizzy with excitement about the chance to work with her.

I'll never forget the scene backstage—there were so many stars coming in and out of her dressing room that I thought I was in country heaven. She was treating me like a mother, introducing me to people, saying, "You've got to meet so-and-so." Toward the end of the night, she said, "There's somebody who'd really like to meet you," and she introduced me to Randy Scruggs. I didn't know who he was until she told me he was the son of Earl Scruggs, the great banjo player. He was kind of sheepishly looking at me and he gave me this song to listen to, and Dottie went back into her mother routine, saying, "You've got to listen to this song," and of course you just didn't say no to Dottie. Well, the song was "Lord, Prepare Me To Be A Sanctuary." I recorded it and it has been one of the biggest songs I've ever had, and after that Randy and I became good friends—all because of my being there with Dottie and knowing enough just to say, "Yes, ma'am."

—**Jessy Dixon, told to Rob Simbeck**

The biggest musical collaboration in Dottie West's life, with Kenny Rogers, happened by accident. Kenny was scheduled for a recording session, but he had gotten the time wrong, and when he went into the studio, Dottie was recording. The two shared a producer, so Kenny stayed and they talked music, and he began singing along with her on the song she was doing, "Every Time Two Fools Collide." Everybody in the studio was so thrilled with the resulting duet that Kenny and Dottie went on to record an album. The song hit #1 on the *Billboard* chart and kicked off a great duet run. They would reach the charts together half a dozen times, with three of those going all the way to the top.

—**Rob Simbeck**

DOTTIE WEST

★★★★★

1932—1991

photo taken 1980

The Whites
★ ★ ★

I've known the Whites since they first came to Nashville, and they're truly like family to me. I've gone on the road with them. We've raised kids together. And to me, the most important thing about the Whites, the unsung heroine, is Patty White, Buck's wife. I loved her to death, and everybody else did too. She and Buck used to sing together—she loved Ralph Stanley and old-time country music—and she taught the girls how to sing harmony. On Friday nights in Arkansas, when the girls were little, they would all drive to the top of the one hill in town where they could pick up WSM. They would take blankets and listen to the Opry, and Sharon has told me, "I can remember lots of nights in that car, going to sleep listening to Roy Acuff sing." Show business wasn't Patty's thing, though. She was a homebody, a great cook who made their house a warm, loving home, and she kept those home fires burning while Buck and the girls were on the road. Sharon would say "She's just too busy," and she was, especially with what she called her "coffee ministry," which was an informal thing where she'd tell people who were troubled to come over and talk it through over a cup of coffee. She might overhear someone in a grocery store talking about something sad, and she'd say, "Here's my phone number. Call me and we can talk this over if you'd like." She was like June Carter, open, and there for you if you needed her. It was Christianity at its best from someone who was never holier-than-thou but who really walked the walk and talked the talk. She had friends all over the country who experienced that, and it was at the core of her family's strength. Buck is a strong, wonderful man, but he relied on Patty so much, and the girls did too.

Her funeral was a classic case of celebrating a life. There was laughter, there were tears, and there was wonderful music, and it's something that continues with the Whites. They're a great family and a joy to be around, and there's a new generation coming along now—Lucas and Molly and Rachel. They're singing together and I hope we have that good Whites/Skaggs harmony for a long time to come, because it's the real deal.

—Keith Bilbrey, told to Rob Simbeck

THE WHITES

★ ★ ★ ★ ★

Cheryl White 1955–, Buck White 1930—,
Sharon White 1953—

photo taken 1984

Wilburn Brothers
★ ★ ★

Johnny Russell made the statement that the Wilburn Brothers (Teddy and Doyle) were the classiest act to ever grace the stage of the Grand Ole Opry. They radiated class and professionalism—they just had it oozing out of them. They had such a phenomenal empire, and helped so many people. Of course, they helped Patty Loveless get started, and they were instrumental in getting both the Osborne Brothers and Loretta Lynn on Decca Records and the Grand Ole Opry. A lot of people have forgotten that the Wilburn Brothers are the ones who really made Loretta's career. They published her songs, managed her, handled her bookings and gave her tremendous exposure on their syndicated television show. The story goes that a song called "I'm Your Favorite Fool" came into their publishing company, Sure-Fire Music. Teddy rewrote the song—Teddy was, in the words of Bill Anderson, "the best 'song doctor' this town ever had"—and it became "Fool Number One." Loretta was new in town and she cut a demo of the song. Doyle and his wife at the time, Margie Bowes, took it to Owen Bradley because they wanted him to hear Loretta sing and hoped to get her onto Decca Records. Owen said, "I like the song but I don't care for the singer. She sounds like Uncle Remus. She's OK but I can't use her. I do want to get the song, though. I promise you I'll take the song and I'll get Brenda Lee to cut it and we'll have a smash hit." Doyle said, "I know you'll have a smash hit, but you don't get the song unless you take the singer with it." Owen reluctantly agreed. Brenda Lee cut "Fool Number One," and it was a tremendous success, and Loretta Lynn got a contract with Decca Records. They were the last of the great brother duet acts, they had an impressive business empire, and they were responsible for launching some of country music's biggest names. They belong in the Country Music Hall of Fame.

—Eddie Stubbs, told to Rob Simbeck

The first "Midnight Jamboree" I did was with the Wilburn Brothers. One night they brought Hoyt Axton, Nicolette Larson and Katy Moffatt, and the whole band, and we sat in that studio and picked music until 5:30 in the morning. I remember they and Hoyt were singing "Streamline Cannonball," the old Roy Acuff song, and they'd get to the chorus and argue about how it went. They never did get the whole song out. I used to love to hear Teddy and Doyle talk about when they first played for Roy Acuff. Their daddy brought them to the backstage door and had them sing for him. Acuff got tears in his eyes, and they were on the show that night, and invited to come to the Opry. They had very humble beginnings and were able to do so much. I still don't think they've gotten the credit they deserve for the people they discovered and encouraged. There were so many, and they were always so good to me.

—Keith Bilbrey, told to Rob Simbeck

WILBURN BROTHERS

★ ★ ★ ★ ★

Virgil Doyle Wilburn 1930—1982
Thurman Theodore "Teddy" Wilburn 1931—2003

photo taken 1979

Bob Wills

★ ★ ★

I had known of Bob Wills since I was a teenager. I really liked him, and used to buy his MGM records. In 1947, I went to San Antonio, Texas to attend photographic school, and while out there, met my wife-to-be, who had moved there from Nashville with her family because of her father's health. Her good friend, who worked with her at the branch office of The National Life and Accident Insurance Company, kept aggravating her to go out with me. She was dating my best friend who lived at the boarding house where I lived. She bugged her until she went on a blind date with me. Dot did not want to go on a blind date. She had already been on one and said she'd never do it again. I had never had a blind date, but I was willing to go along with it. Well, the crowd at our boarding house knew that Bob Wills was going to be playing at the Olmos club, which was a very popular music club in San Antonio. When Dot got the word that we were going out to hear Bob Wills, she asked, "Who is Bob Wills?" She didn't realize that while in Texas, you do not ask who Bob Wills is. She found out when she went with me and our entire crowd to that wonderful dance party. We went out for Mexican that night after the show, and probably didn't come in until 3 a.m. Dot has now been my wife for over 50 years. And, she loves Bob Wills' music as much as I do.

—Les Leverett, told to Libby Leverett-Crew

I was always fascinated by my Daddy's stories about growing up in Hall County, Texas. His stories had a cast of colorful characters that I had never met, like Uncle Blue Eye and Uncle Pink. I used to get it confused and ask about Uncle Pink Eye!

When my siblings were off being teenagers and young adults, it was just me and my parents at home. I had been sick with pneumonia when I was two, and he always called me "Half Pint" and "Little Bit." The Texas Playboys knew me as the daughter who wouldn't give her father kisses until he shaved (he had a heavy five o'clock shadow that hurt my face). I remember being so proud of the first pair of cowboy boots he bought me, and I remember my very first board game, which he bought me at the airport in Las Vegas—it was a toy roulette wheel! No "Candy Land" for this little girl. Later I had a horse racing game that I loved.

When I was 14, my father suffered a disabling stroke, and I remember the hundreds of letters from his fans. We had to use large plastic trash bags to hold them all. I began to read them and I learned what my father meant to his audience. It was a revelation to me. My own favorite memory of him is the way he looked before he would leave for his Saturday night television broadcast. He smelled like "English Leather," his suit was perfect, his hat was pure white and his black boots shone—and his face was soft from shaving when I would kiss his cheek "good-bye."

—Cindy Wills

BOB WILLS

★★★★★

1905—1975

photo taken 1968

Mac Wiseman

★ ★ ★

Mac had polio as a youngster, but it had a positive effect: "It took me a little longer," he laughs in retrospect, "but I could throw as much hay as any of the others and I learned to stay with the job 'til it was done." He came through polio with a limp, but there was obviously no damage to his hands or his vocal chords. Mac developed a commanding style on guitar and a soulful, haunting style of singing. Although he's primarily identified with bluegrass, and appropriately so, Mac recorded a stirring rendition of "Springtime In The Rockies" with full strings in the '60s, and has served in management, production, and as an example to musicians for "putting something back" into the business.

—**Bill Littleton**

Mac was the first country music artist I ever saw perform live. I couldn't have been older than four or five. He came with Carl Story to the Putnam County Courthouse. That was the only place people could gather, and he and Carl sang up by the judge's desk, and I just fell in love with him then. I never dreamed that someday he and I would become friends. We did, though, so when I was asked to be the grand marshall of the Cookeville Christmas Parade a few years ago, I called him. I said, "Mac, I'm doing this Christmas parade and I would love for you to go with me. We'll circle that very courthouse where I saw you for the first time." He cut short a trip to Jeckyll Island, where they have the big bluegrass festival, to come and do it with me, and I'll never forget it as long as I live. Before the show we went to eat and came back by my mother and father's house. He was my dad's very favorite singer of all time, and he brought his guitar in and sat at my mother and daddy's kitchen table and sang. That was something my dad would never forget. I remember my son Eric, who was five or six at the time, wanted him to do "The Ballad of Davy Crockett," and Mac said, "Well, Eric, I don't think I can remember the words to that." Eric said, "Well, I know it. You just sing it." And little Eric sat there and fed him the words to "Davy Crockett" so he could sing it. I love that man, and we've had a lot of good times down through the years. I walk in a room and when I see Mac, it's like, "Everything's OK."

—**Keith Bilbrey, told to Rob Simbeck**

MAC WISEMAN

★★★★★

1925—

photo taken 1978

Tammy Wynette
★★★

I was working on a new album with producer Billy Sherrill, planning the project, listening to hundreds of songs, and just hanging out in Billy's small Epic Records office. I had noticed, on my way in, a pale, thin, shy-looking blonde in the receptionist's office, holding tightly to a recording tape box. I thought she was just there visiting with Billy's secretary Nancy. We killed a couple of hours in his office, and as I stepped out later to go to the bathroom I noticed the blonde girl was still sitting there, and I asked Billy who she was. He said he didn't know her, that she had just walked in and said she needed to talk to Billy, and that she was from Alabama. We worked on the songs another hour, and finally Billy said, "Well, let's bring her in and see what she wants." She came into the office and just handed the tape to Billy without much fanfare. He threaded it onto his tape machine, punched the button, and one of the greatest female voices of all time started singing, "Just follow the stairway to apartment #9." It was chill-bump city, friends. The look on Billy's face was marvelous to behold because he practiced being Mr. Poker Face. But not this time. Miss Tammy, the hairdresser from Alabama, had just blown the socks off of Mr. Sherrill and had blown me completely away. Musical history was about to me made with the partnership of the intense, introspective producer and the shy, beautiful lady with the God-gifted voice. It was a special moment to witness the meeting.

—**Stan Hitchcock, from** *At The Corner of Music Row and Memory Lane*

When Tammy released her *Without Walls* album of duets, an Australian couple won the opportunity to have dinner with her. The timing didn't work out, so Tammy invited them to have lunch at her house, and she asked me to help break the ice. We had lunch, and then Tammy gave us a tour of the house, which Hank Williams had once owned. It was incredible, with a huge great room and a master bathroom with the biggest bathtub I have ever seen—it looked like a small swimming pool—and a beautician's chair. Tammy had jeans and a sweater on, and she did her best to make them feel at home. What struck me was that it was the same way she treated everybody. This was a legend, someone idolized by many of the people she recorded those duets with. When she called Wynonna to ask if she'd do a song with her, for instance, Wynonna danced around her hotel bed in excitement. I traveled with Tammy to New York, and whether she was with diehard fans or other artists, she was gracious in every situation, wanting to make sure everybody felt comfortable and at ease.

—**Craig Campbell**

TAMMY WYNETTE

1942—1998

photo taken 1981